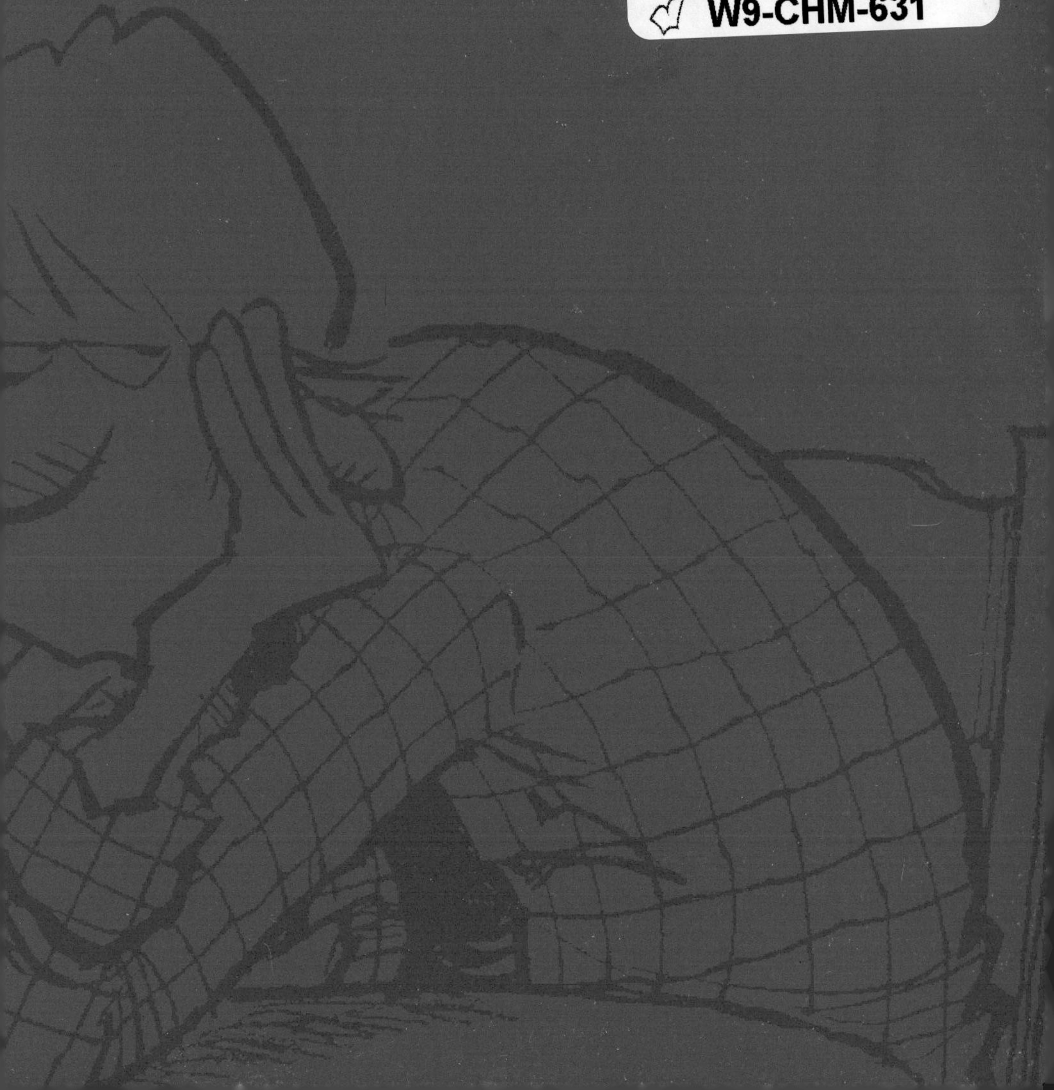

A **Zits**® GUIDE to
LIVING WITH YOUR TEENAGER

ALSO BY JERRY SCOTT and JIM BORGMAN

Zits: Sketchbook 1
Growth Spurt: Zits Sketchbook 2
Don't Roll Your Eyes at Me, Young Man!: Zits Sketchbook 3
Are We an "Us"?: Zits Sketchbook 4
Zits Unzipped: Zits Sketchbook 5
Busted!: Zits Sketchbook 6
Road Trip: Zits Sketchbook 7
Teenage Tales: Zits Sketchbook No. 8
Thrashed: Zits Sketchbook No. 9
Pimp My Lunch: Zits Sketchbook No. 10
Are We Out of the Driveway Yet?: Zits Sketchbook No. 11
Rude, Crude, and Tattooed: Zits Sketchbook No. 12
Pierced
Lust and Other Uses for Spare Hormones

TREASURIES

Humongous Zits
Big Honkin' Zits
Zits: Supersized
Random Zits
Crack of Noon
Alternative Zits
Jeremy and Mom
My Bad

A *Zits* GUIDE to LIVING WITH YOUR TEENAGER

by Jerry Scott
and Jim Borgman

**Andrews McMeel
Publishing, LLC**
Kansas City • Sydney • London

Zits® is syndicated internationally by King Features Syndicate, Inc. For information, write King Features Syndicate, Inc., 300 West Fifty-Seventh Street, New York, New York 10019.

10 11 12 13 14 WKT 10 9 8 7 6 5 4 3 2 1

ISBN-13: 978-0-7407-9168-0
ISBN-10: 0-7407-9168-0

Library of Congress Control Number: 2009939465

Zits® may be viewed online at
www.kingfeatures.com.

www.andrewsmcmeel.com

Introduction

I was attending a party one night when a bedraggled-looking neighbor staggered up to me. His hair was askew, his shirttail hung loose, and he had the shell-shocked look in his eyes that you see in some WWII veterans when you mention the beaches of Anzio.

"If you ever want to do another comic strip," he said in a raspy voice that invoked unspeakable horrors, "do one about teenagers."

Any subject so terrifying must be equal parts funny, I figured, and on that premise Jim Borgman and I sat down and created *Zits*. It is intended as our daily "message in a bottle" sent to those poor souls marooned on the desert islands of teenager parenthood. You wouldn't believe how many e-mails we get saying, "Thank God! I thought we were alone!"

Here, a dozen years later, is a gift for my old shell-shocked neighbor, wherever he and his wife may be. *A Zits Guide to Living with Your Teenager* is all you need to navigate the straits of the teenage years—along with a self-restocking refrigerator, a standard-issue cattle prod, and a barrel of whatever transforms your blackest nightmares to distant happy memories.

Jerry Scott

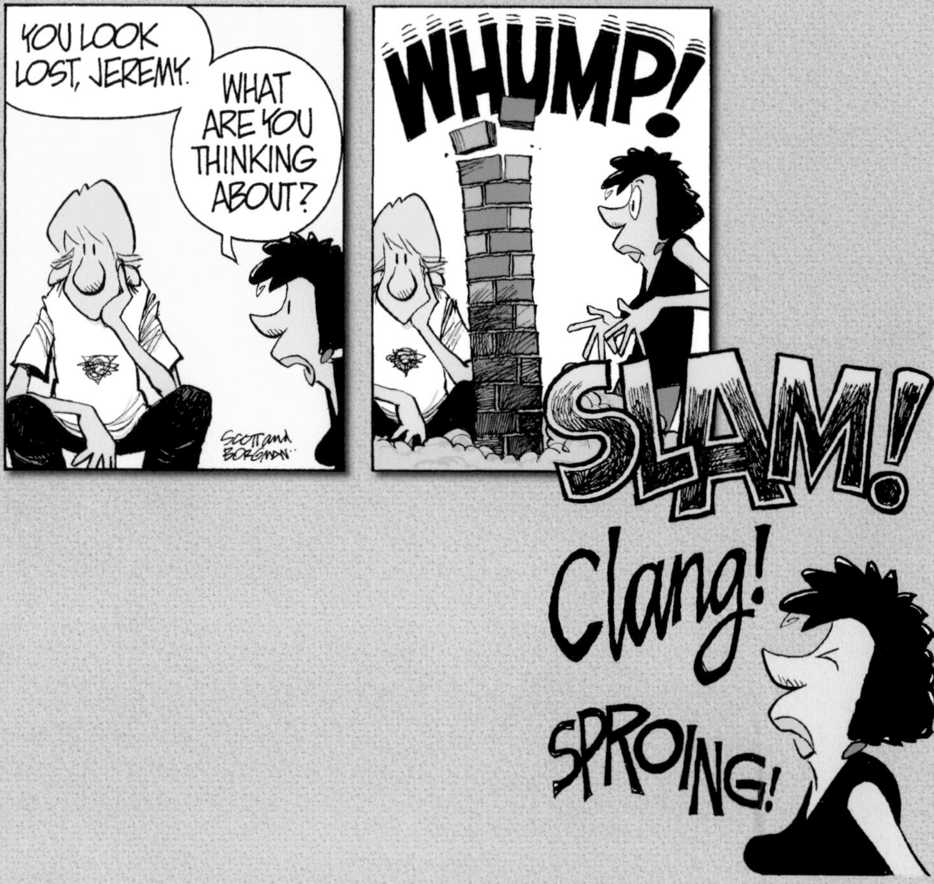
YOU LOOK LOST, JEREMY.
WHAT ARE YOU THINKING ABOUT?
SCOTT and BORGMAN
WHUMP!
SLAM!
Clang!
SPROING!

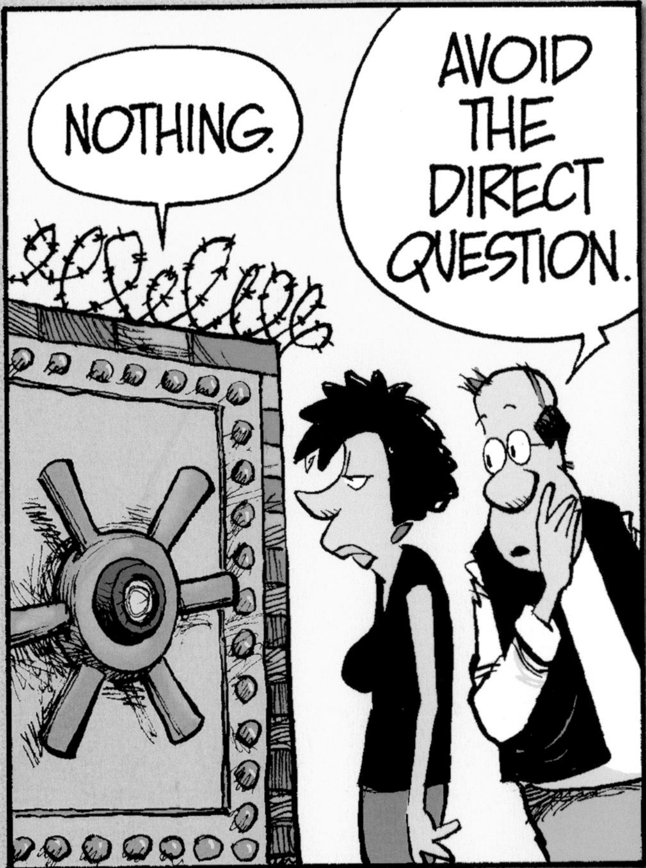
NOTHING.
AVOID THE DIRECT QUESTION.

Lesson One.

MOM? DAD?
THERE'S SOMETHING I REALLY NEED TO TALK TO YOU ABOUT...
...BUT I PROBABLY WON'T.

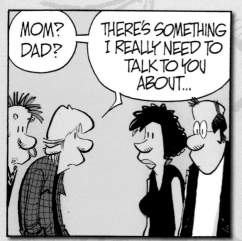

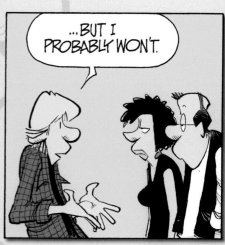

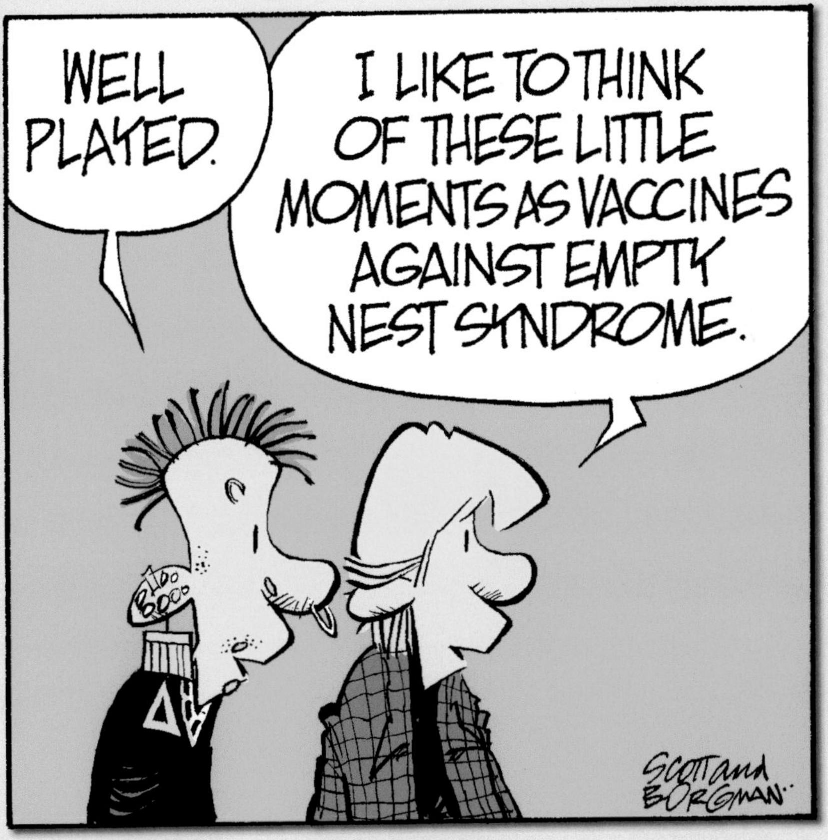
WELL PLAYED.
I LIKE TO THINK OF THESE LITTLE MOMENTS AS VACCINES AGAINST EMPTY NEST SYNDROME.
SCOTT and BORGMAN

The lack of communication can be both a symptom and a sport.

JEREMY, LET ME TELL YOU A LITTLE STORY ABOUT PATIENCE...
IS IT LONG?
CAN YOU JUST GIVE ME THE BULLET POINTS?
OR MAYBE THE HIGHLIGHTS?
A SHORT SYNOPSIS WOULD PROBABLY BE MORE EFFECTIVE.
SCOTT and BORGMAN

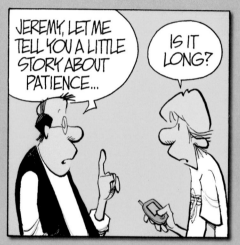

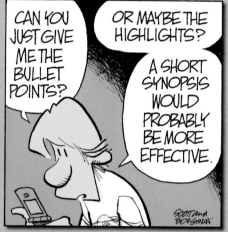

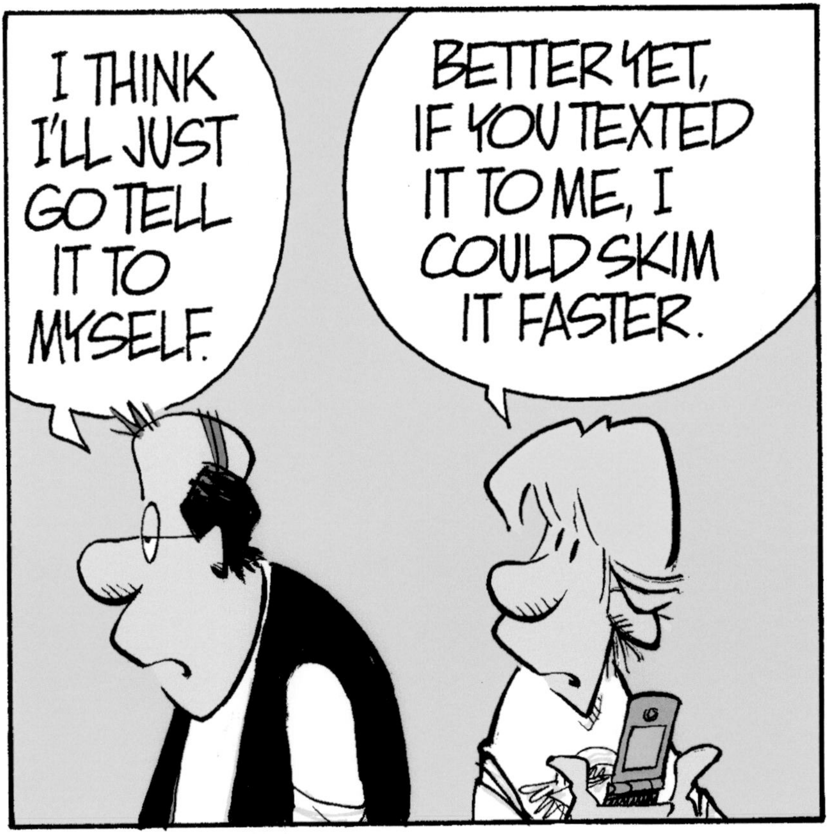
I THINK I'LL JUST GO TELL IT TO MYSELF.
BETTER YET, IF YOU TEXTED IT TO ME, I COULD SKIM IT FASTER.

Compress all of your accumulated wisdom and e-mail it as an attachment.

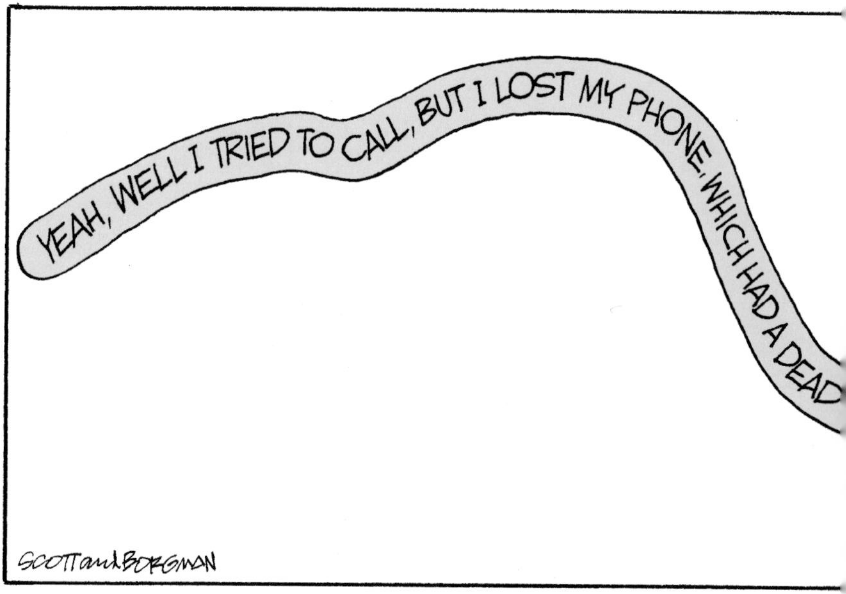
YEAH, WELL I TRIED TO CALL, BUT I LOST MY PHONE, WHICH HAD A DEAD
SCOTT and BORGMAN

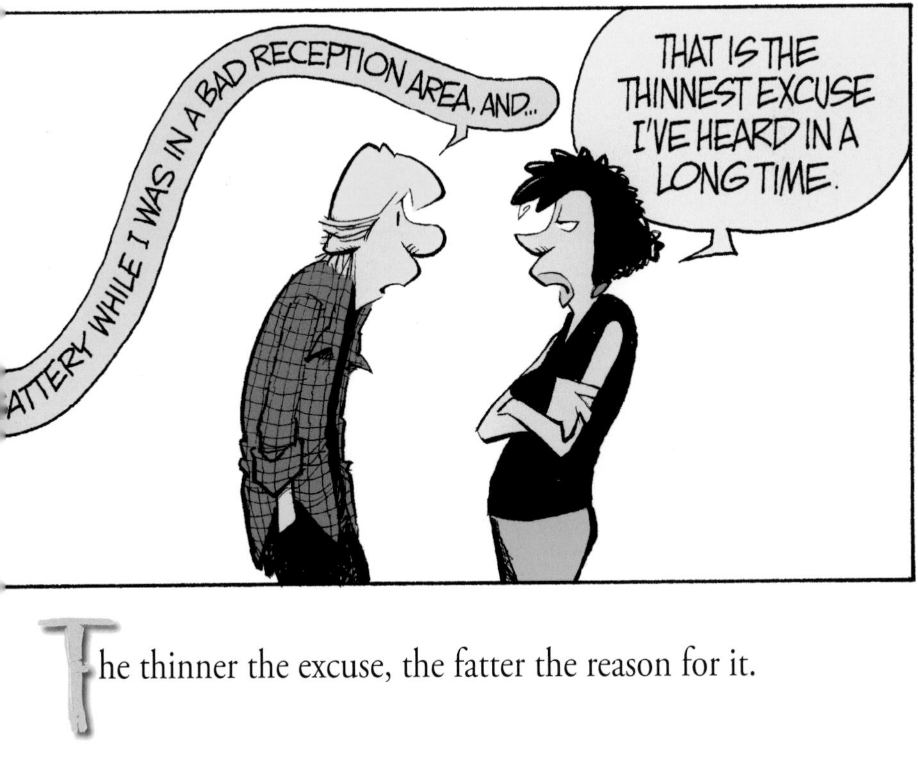
ATTERY WHILE I WAS IN A BAD RECEPTION AREA, AND...
THAT IS THE THINNEST EXCUSE I'VE HEARD IN A LONG TIME.

The thinner the excuse, the fatter the reason for it.

HA! HA! HA! HA! HA! HA! HA!
SCOTT and BORGMAN

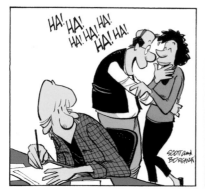

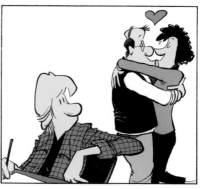

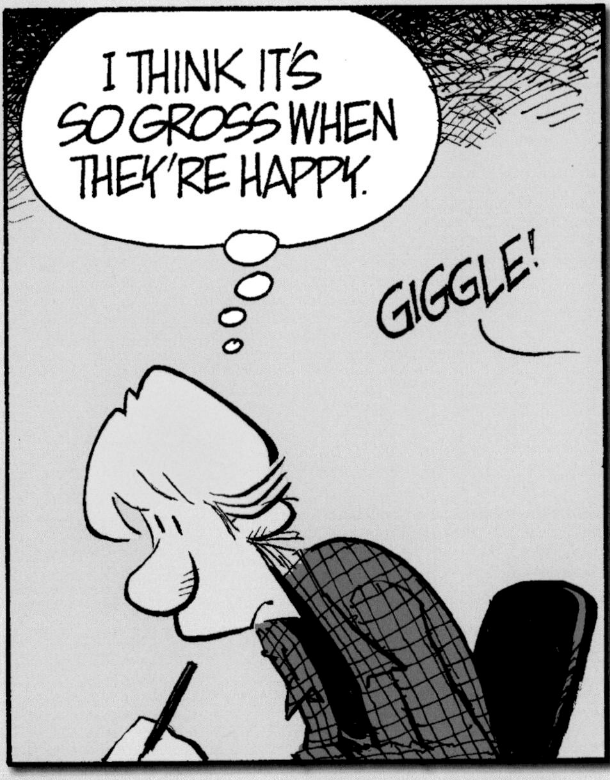
I THINK IT'S SO GROSS WHEN THEY'RE HAPPY.
GIGGLE!

Relish your new role as a profound embarrassment to your teenager.

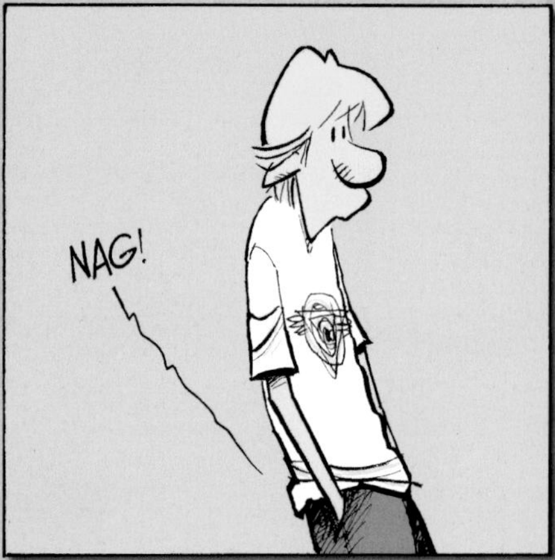
NAG!

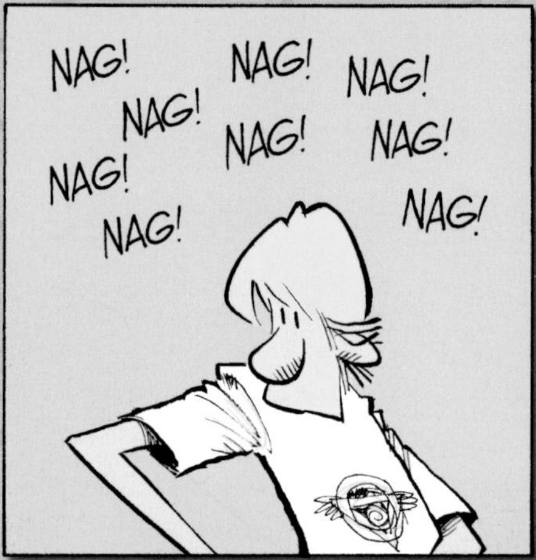
NAG!
NAG!
NAG!
NAG!
NAG!
NAG!
NAG!
NAG!
NAG!

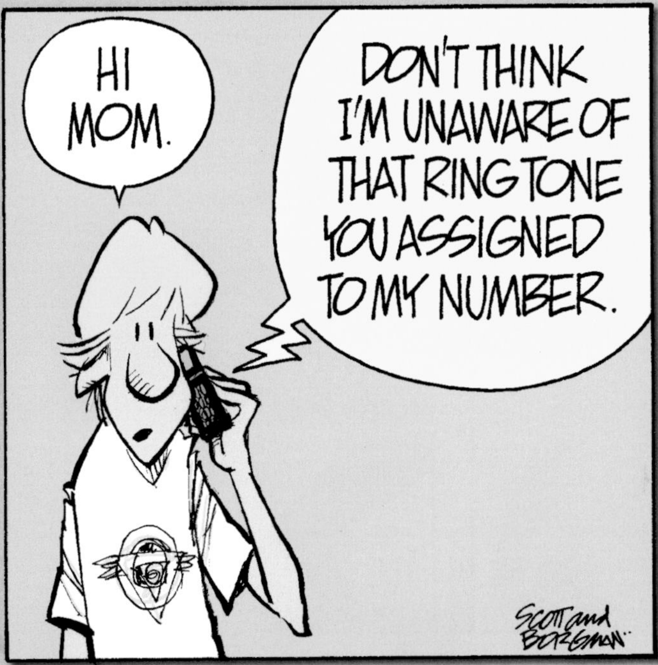
HI MOM.
DON'T THINK I'M UNAWARE OF THAT RING TONE YOU ASSIGNED TO MY NUMBER.
SCOTT and BORGMAN

Forget any dreams you ever had of being "the cool parent."

MOM!
MOM!

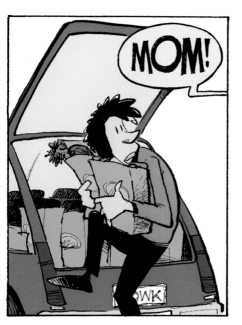

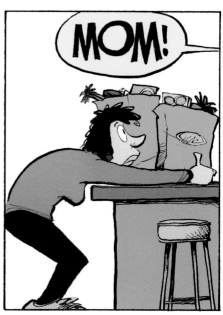

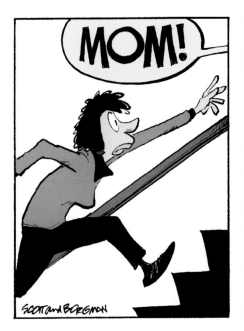

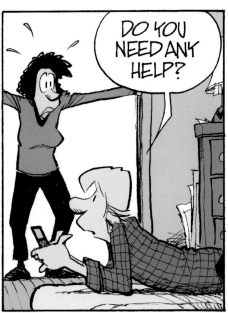

MOM!
DO YOU NEED ANY HELP?
SCOTT and BORGMAN

Accept any offer of help, no matter how unhelpful it is.

I OFTEN FIND MYSELF THINKING THAT THE WORLD IS STARTING TO MOVE TOO FAST FOR ME.
REALLY? I'M LISTENING TO A DIFFERENT iPOD IN EACH EAR WHILE WE'RE HAVING THIS CONVERSATION AND I'M STILL BORED TO TEARS.

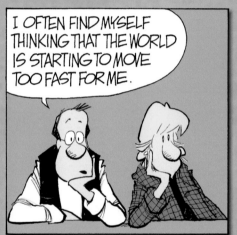

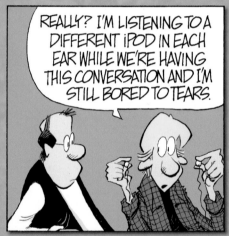

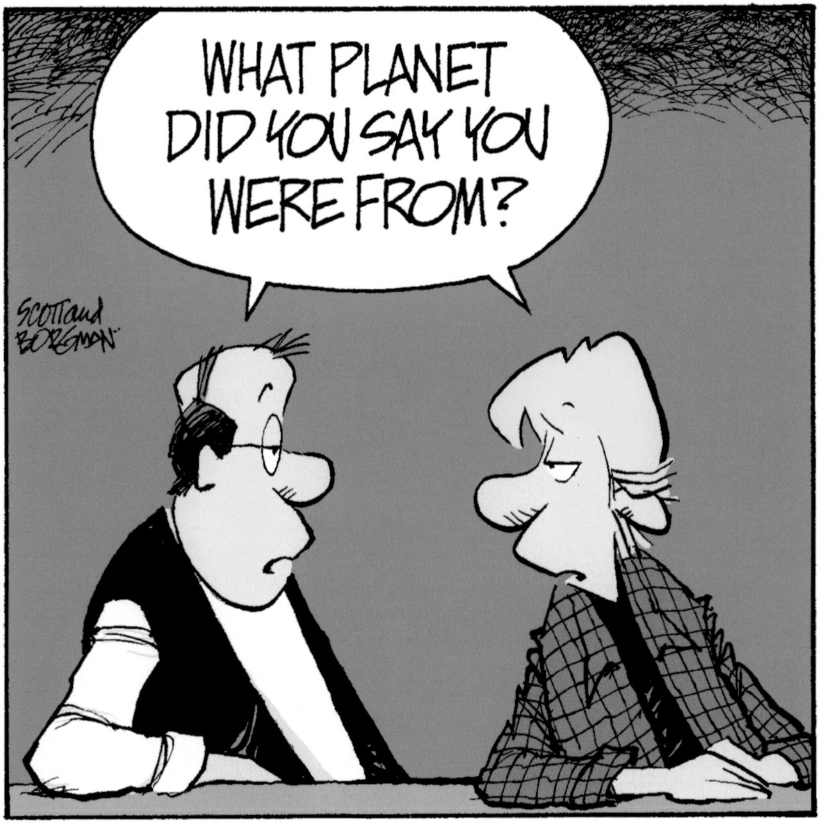
WHAT PLANET DID YOU SAY YOU WERE FROM?
SCOTT and BORGMAN

They're not ignoring you. They don't even see you.

JEREMY HAS BEEN IN HIS ROOM SINCE HE CAME HOME.
I'M WORRIED.
DID HE SAY ANYTHING?
HE SAID THERE WAS NOTHING WRONG!
SCOTT and BORGMAN

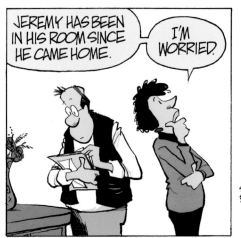

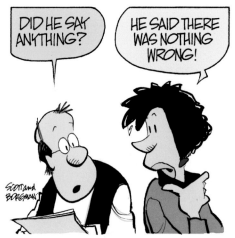

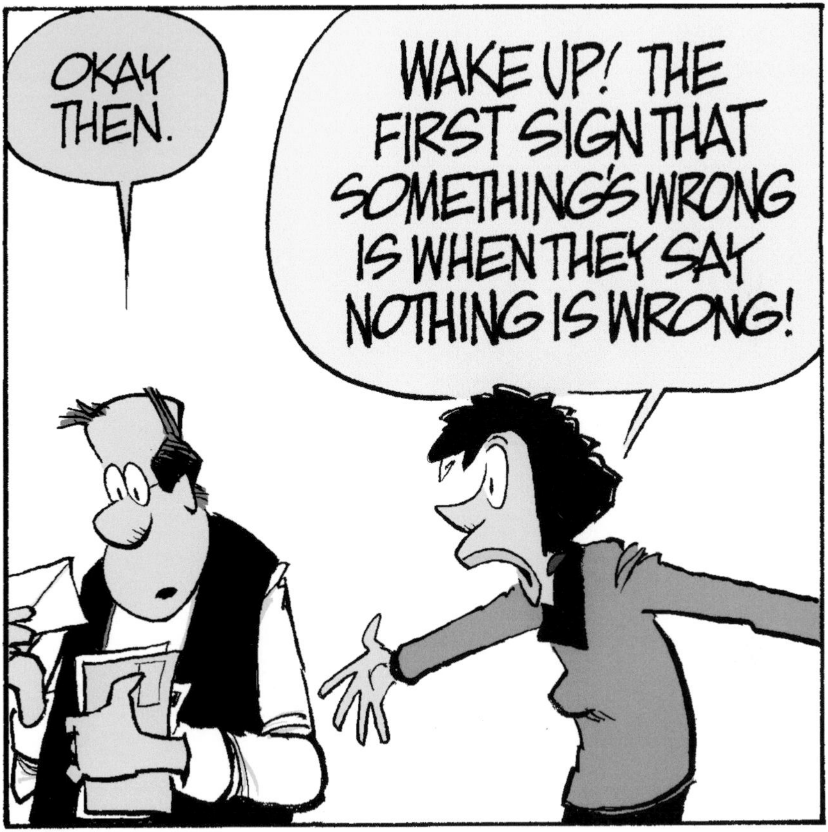
OKAY THEN.
WAKE UP! THE FIRST SIGN THAT SOMETHING'S WRONG IS WHEN THEY SAY NOTHING IS WRONG!

The teen years are a worry marathon. Pace yourself, and drink lots of water.

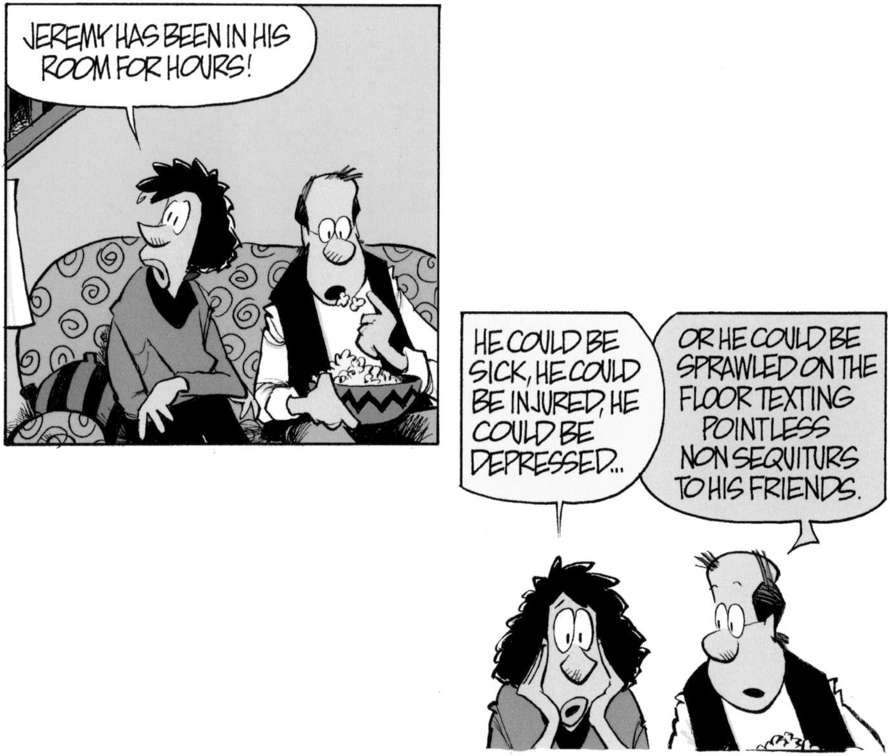
JEREMY HAS BEEN IN HIS ROOM FOR HOURS!
HE COULD BE SICK, HE COULD BE INJURED, HE COULD BE DEPRESSED...
OR HE COULD BE SPRAWLED ON THE FLOOR TEXTING POINTLESS NON SEQUITURS TO HIS FRIENDS.

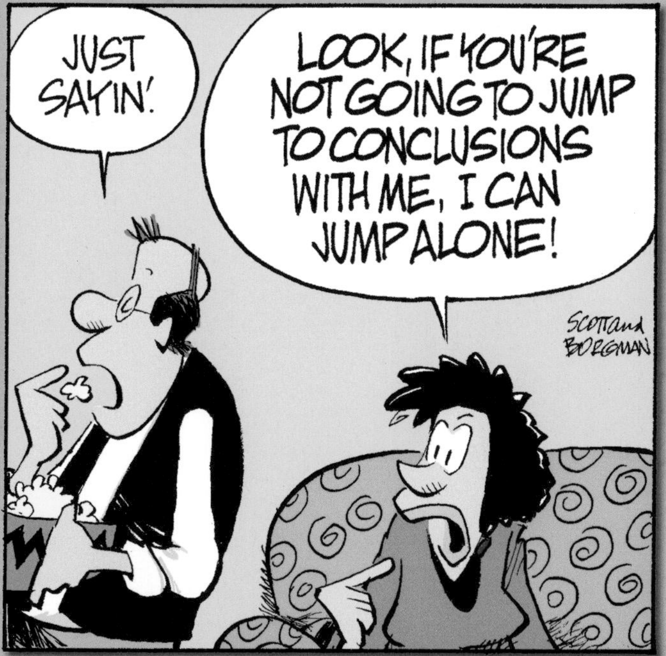
JUST SAYIN'.
LOOK, IF YOU'RE NOT GOING TO JUMP TO CONCLUSIONS WITH ME, I CAN JUMP ALONE!
SCOTT and BORGMAN

You have entered the Forbidden Kingdom of Worry. You are the master of all the worry you survey. You are one with the worry.

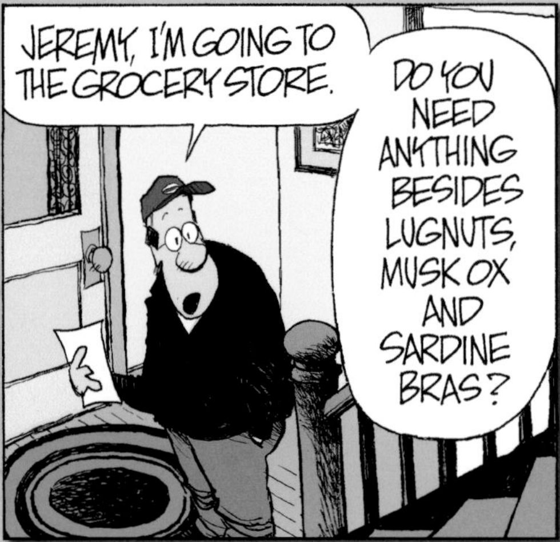
JEREMY, I'M GOING TO THE GROCERY STORE.
DO YOU NEED ANYTHING BESIDES LUGNUTS, MUSK OX AND SARDINE BRAS?

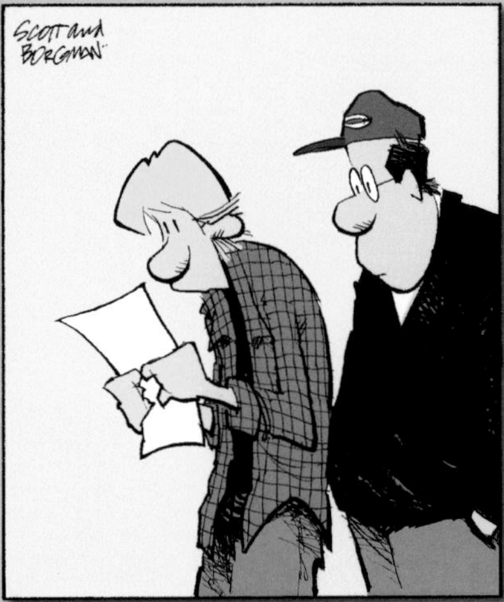
SCOTT and BORGMAN

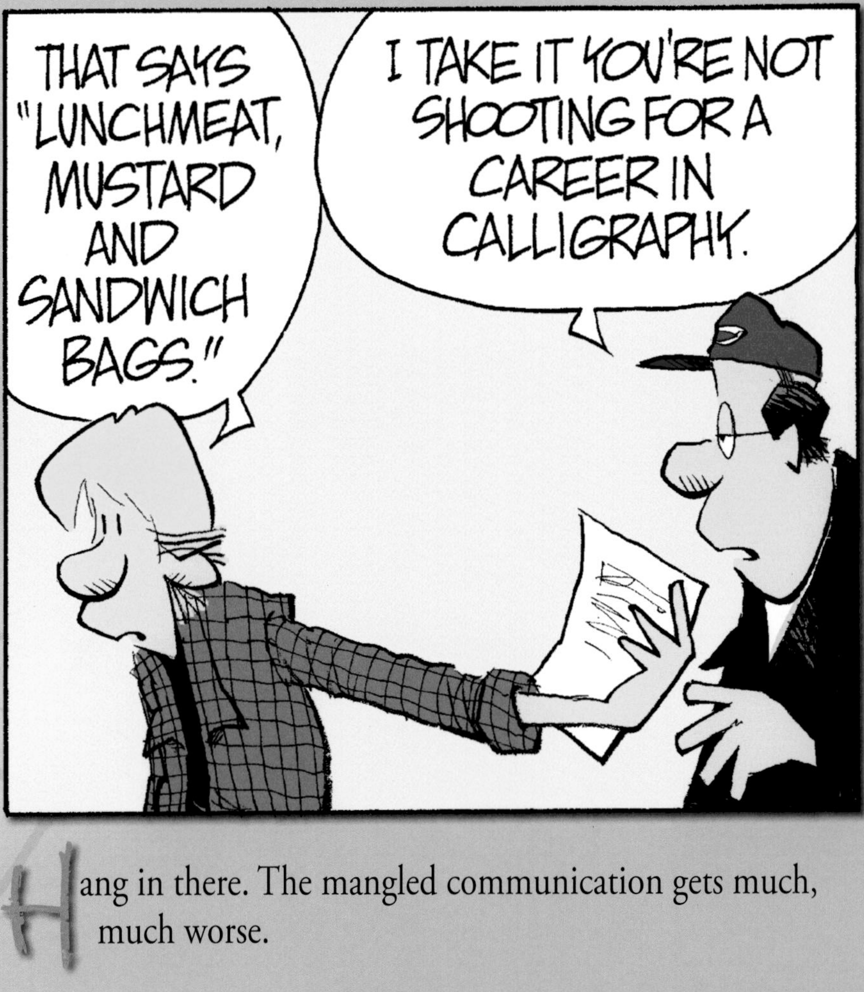
THAT SAYS "LUNCHMEAT, MUSTARD AND SANDWICH BAGS."
I TAKE IT YOU'RE NOT SHOOTING FOR A CAREER IN CALLIGRAPHY.

Hang in there. The mangled communication gets much, much worse.

JEREMY, CAN I HAVE FIVE MINUTES OF YOUR TIME?
WHAT FOR?
TO TALK
ABOUT LIFE
YOU KNOW... LOVE, DEATH, CAREER, MARRIAGE...

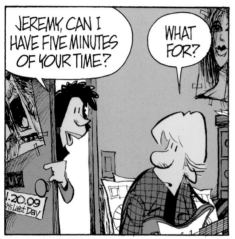

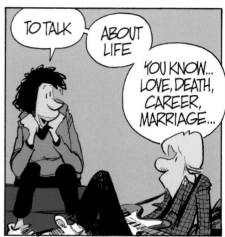

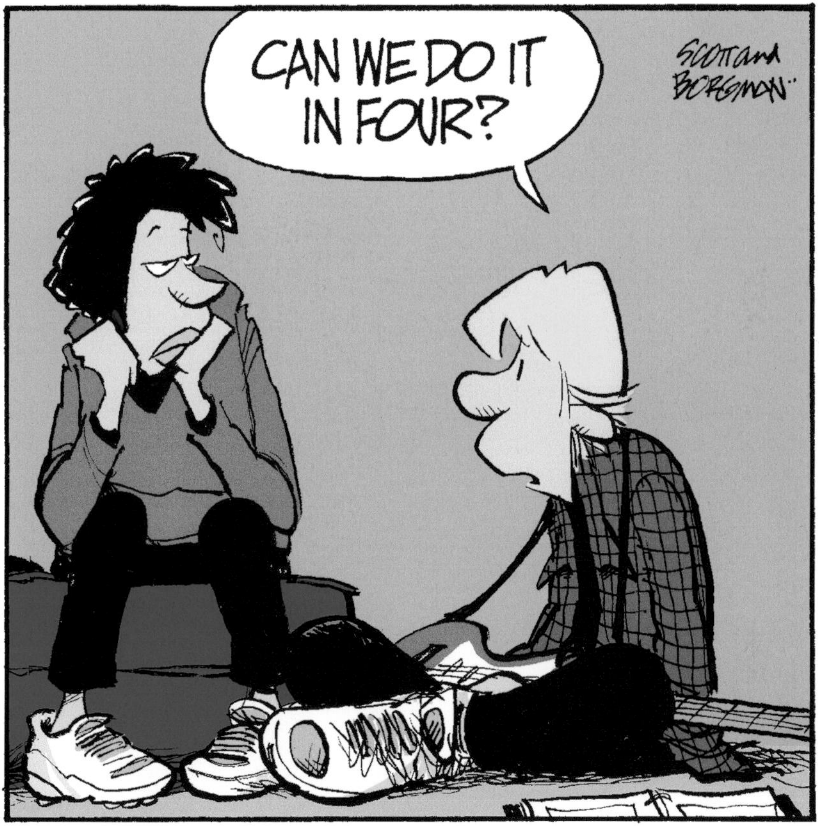
CAN WE DO IT IN FOUR?
SCOTT and BORGMAN

When you're a teenager, a minute represents a larger percentage of your life.

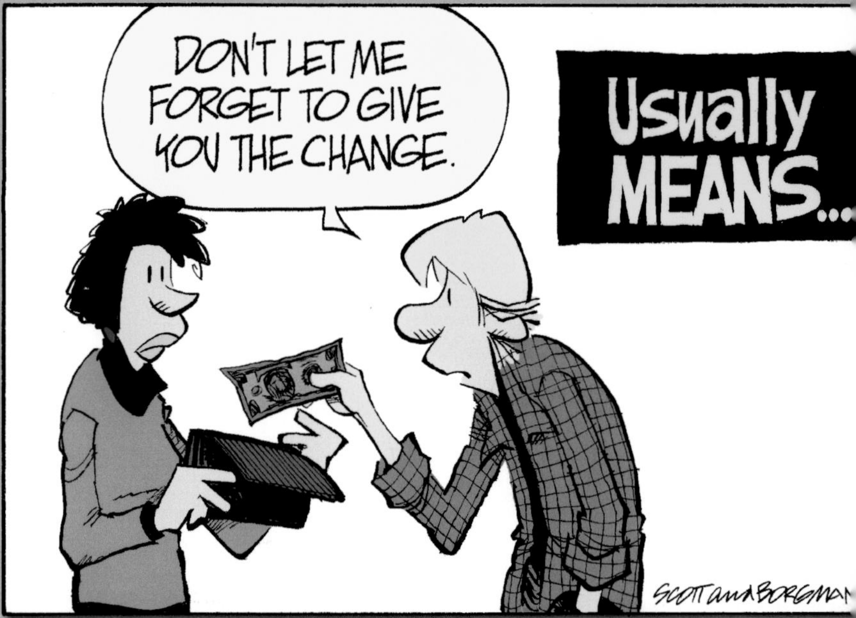
DON'T LET ME FORGET TO GIVE YOU THE CHANGE.
Usually MEANS...
SCOTT and BORGMAN

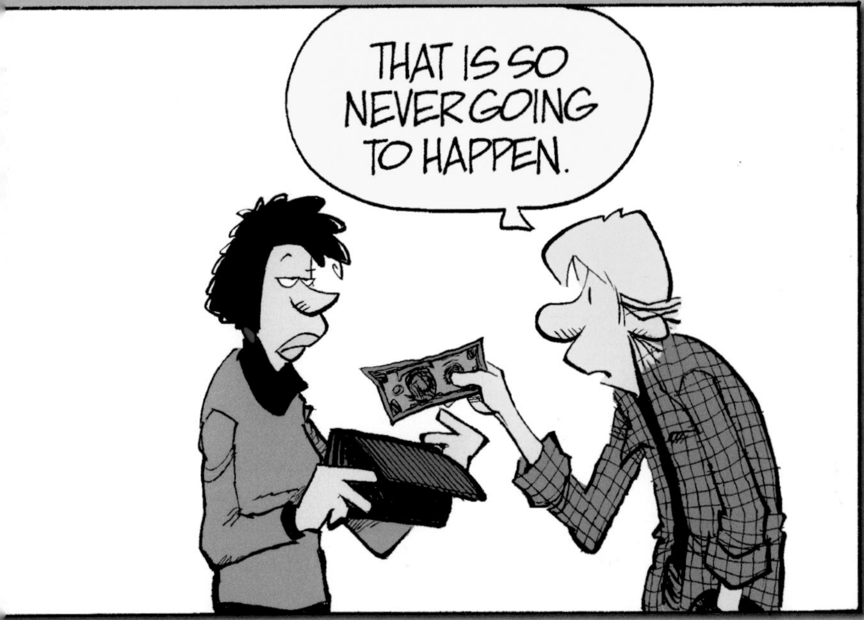
THAT IS SO NEVER GOING TO HAPPEN.

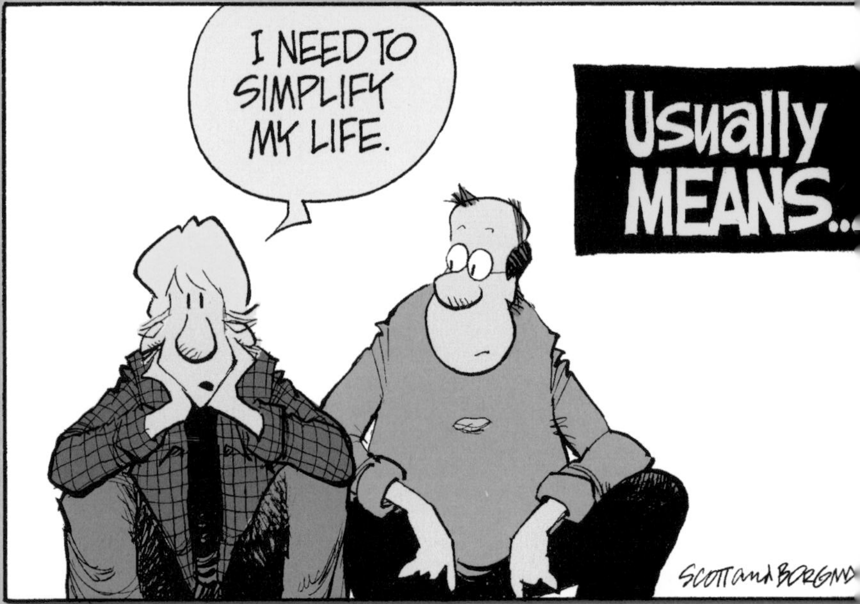
I NEED TO SIMPLIFY MY LIFE.
Usually MEANS...
SCOTT and BORGMAN

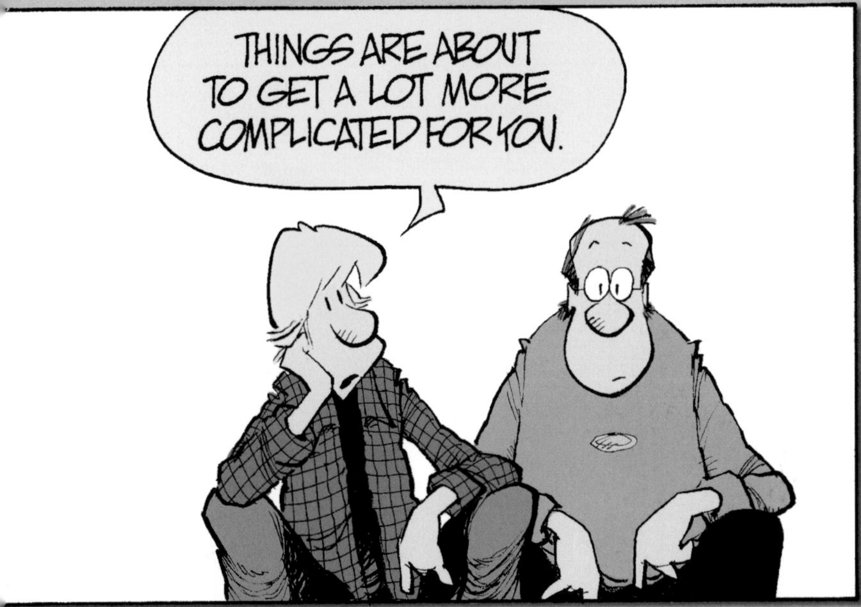
THINGS ARE ABOUT TO GET A LOT MORE COMPLICATED FOR YOU.

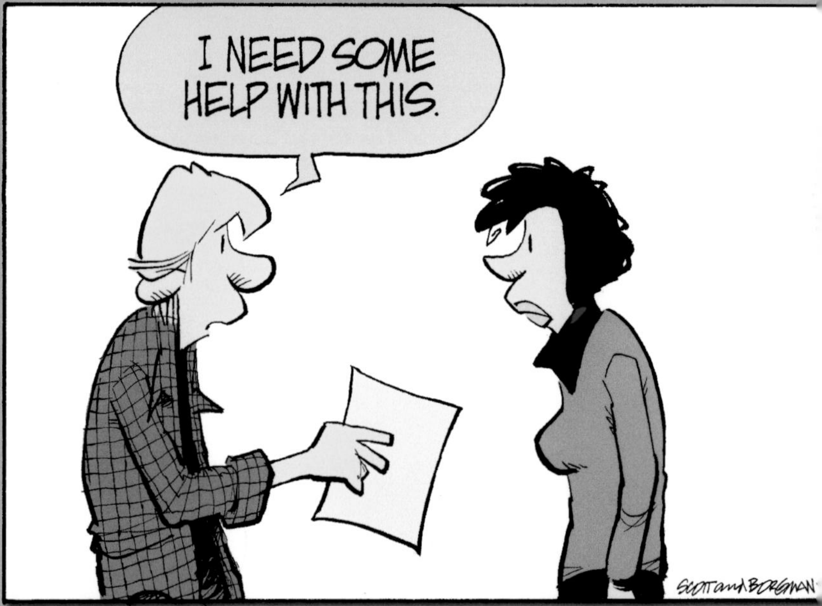
I NEED SOME HELP WITH THIS.
SCOTT and BORGMAN

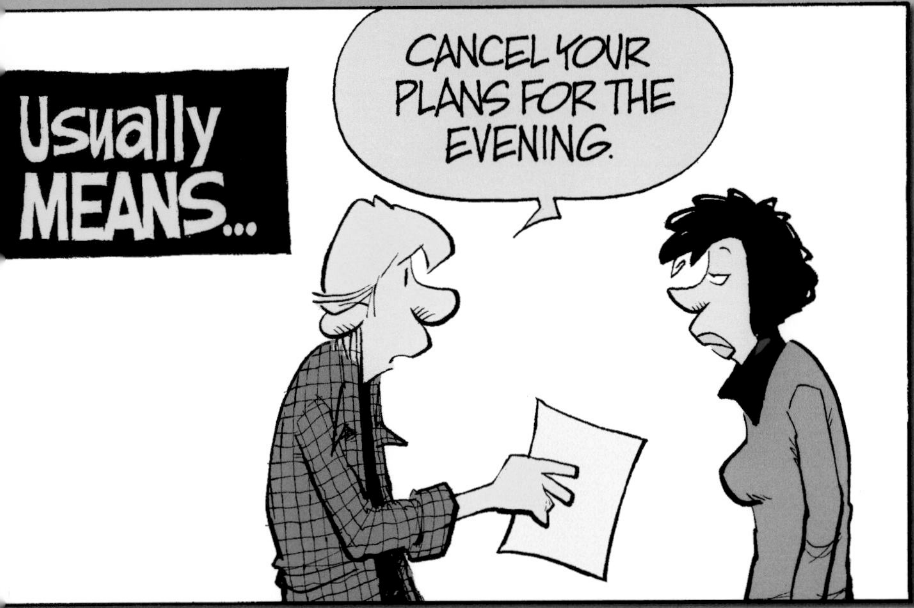
Usually MEANS...
CANCEL YOUR PLANS FOR THE EVENING.

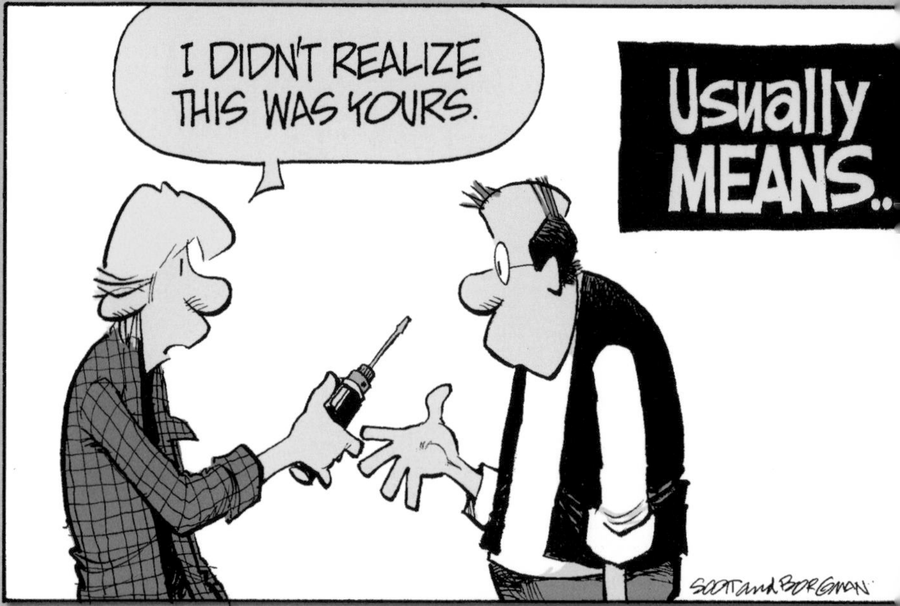
I DIDN'T REALIZE THIS WAS YOURS.
Usually MEANS..
SCOTT and BORGMAN

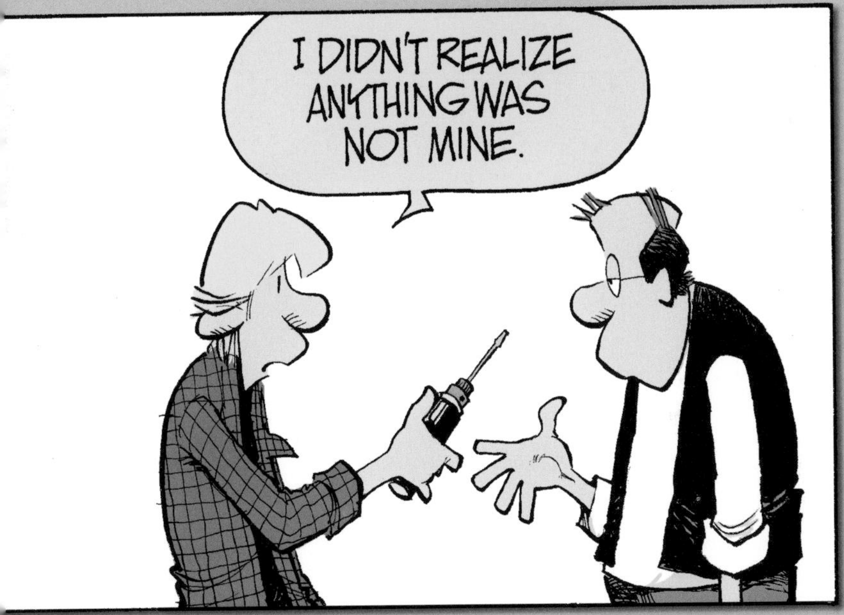
I DIDN'T REALIZE ANYTHING WAS NOT MINE.

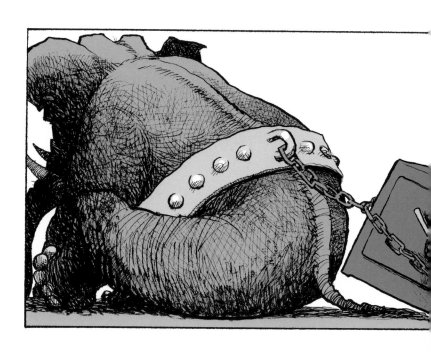

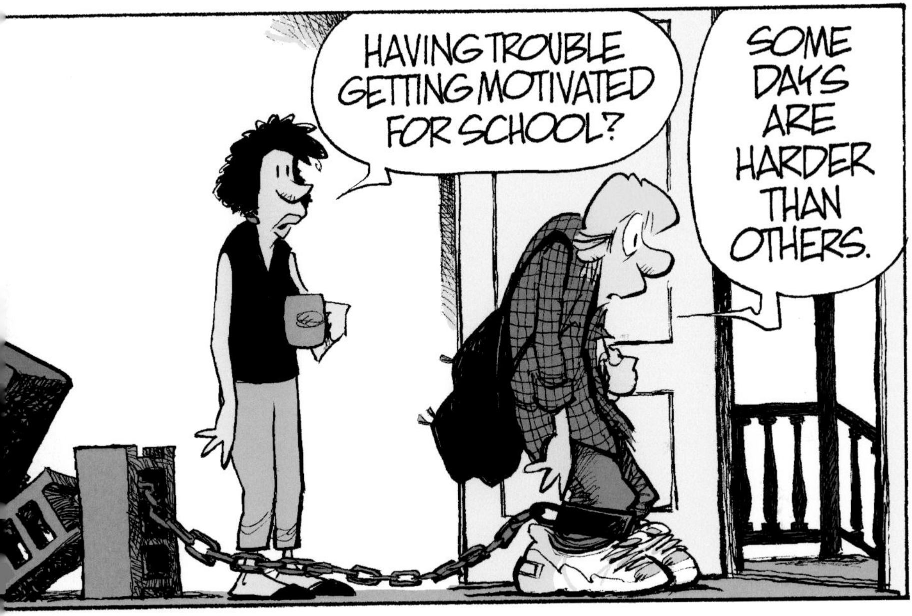
HAVING TROUBLE GETTING MOTIVATED FOR SCHOOL?
SOME DAYS ARE HARDER THAN OTHERS.

Be understanding. Adolescence is a backbreaking job with no vacation.

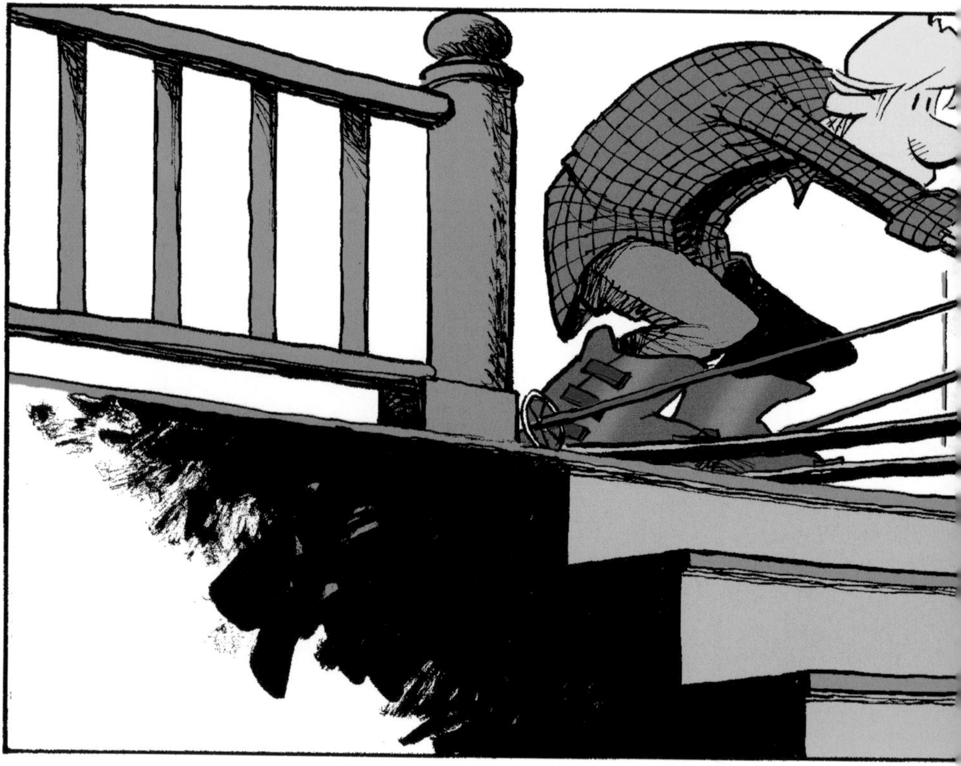

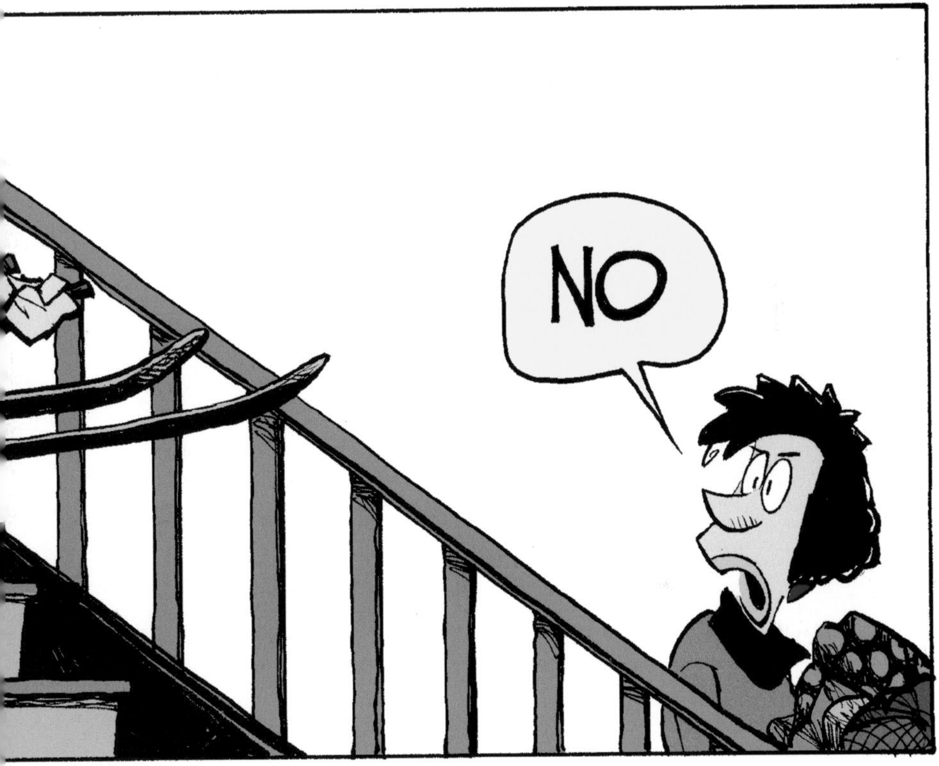
NO

As a graduate of Teenage Knucklehead University, remember to be patient with the current student body.

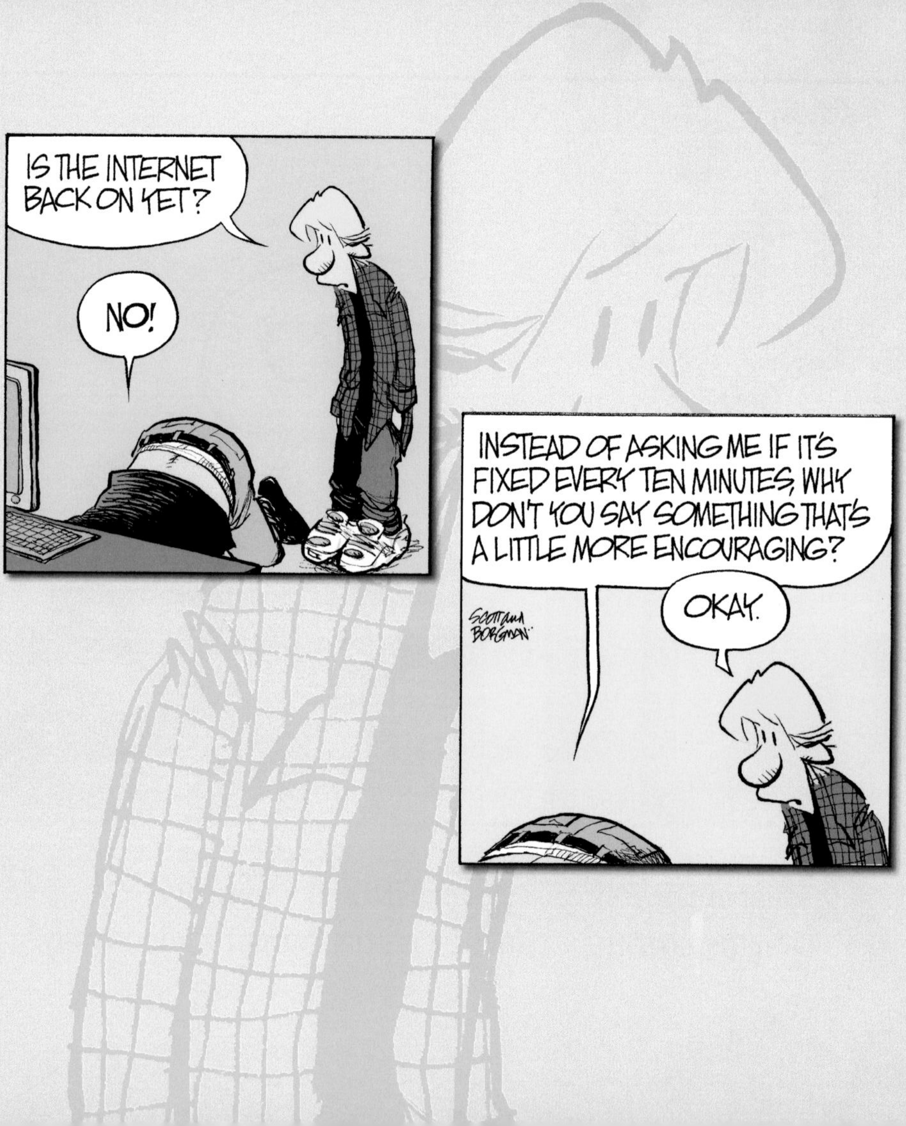
IS THE INTERNET BACK ON YET?
NO!
INSTEAD OF ASKING ME IF IT'S FIXED EVERY TEN MINUTES, WHY DON'T YOU SAY SOMETHING THAT'S A LITTLE MORE ENCOURAGING?
OKAY.

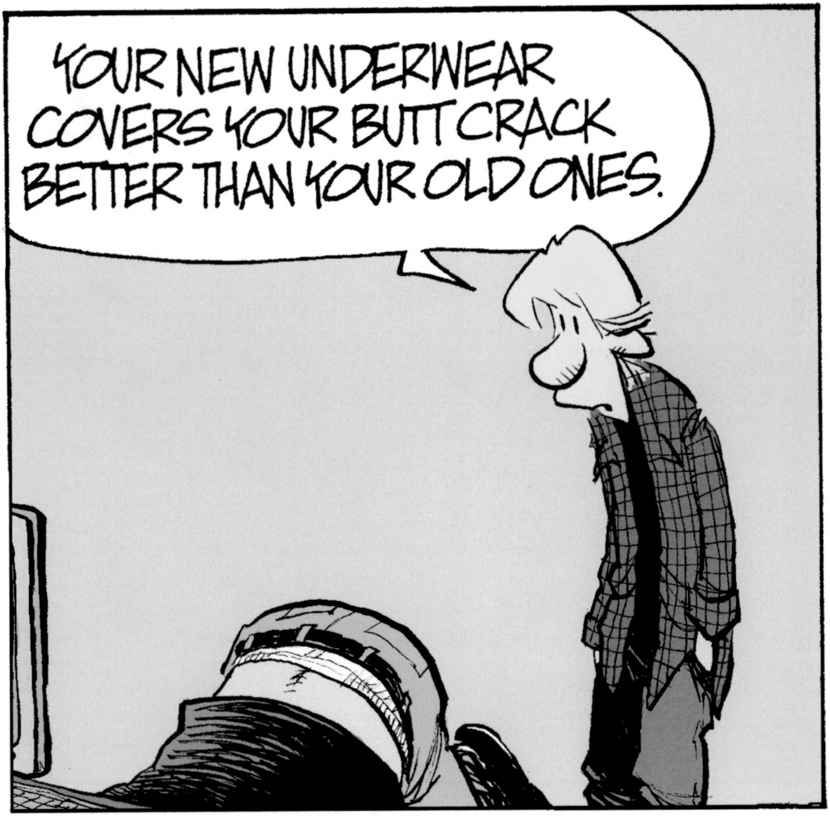
YOUR NEW UNDERWEAR COVERS YOUR BUTT CRACK BETTER THAN YOUR OLD ONES.

Accept anything resembling a compliment.

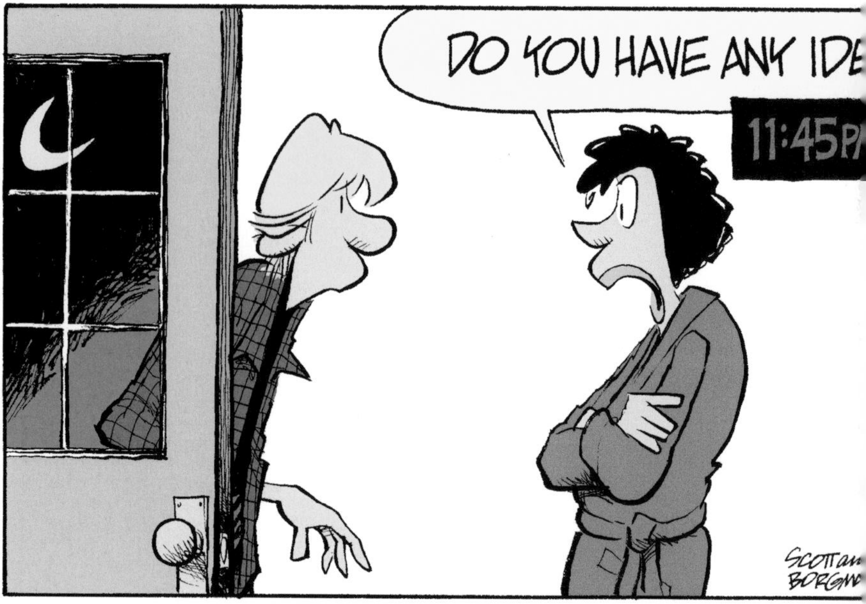
DO YOU HAVE ANY IDE
11:45P
SCOTT an
BORGMA

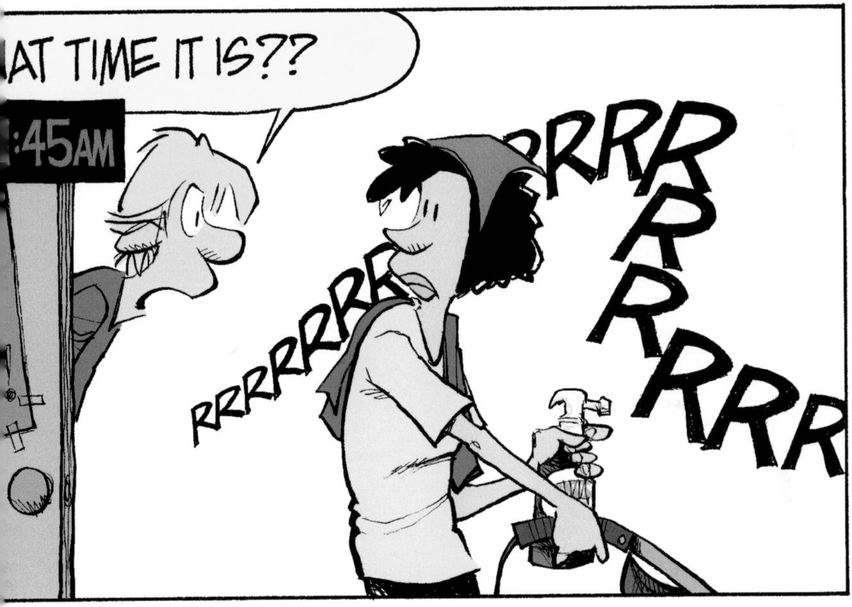
AT TIME IT IS??
:45AM
RRRRRRR
RRRR
RRRRRRR

Remember, in the world of teenagers, daylight is irrelevant.

WHERE'S MY $17 CHANGE?
PROBABLY IN MY BACKPACK.

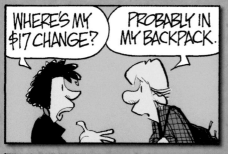

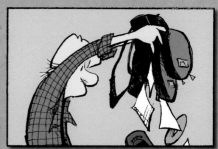

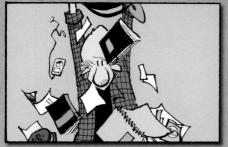

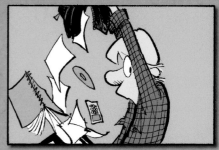

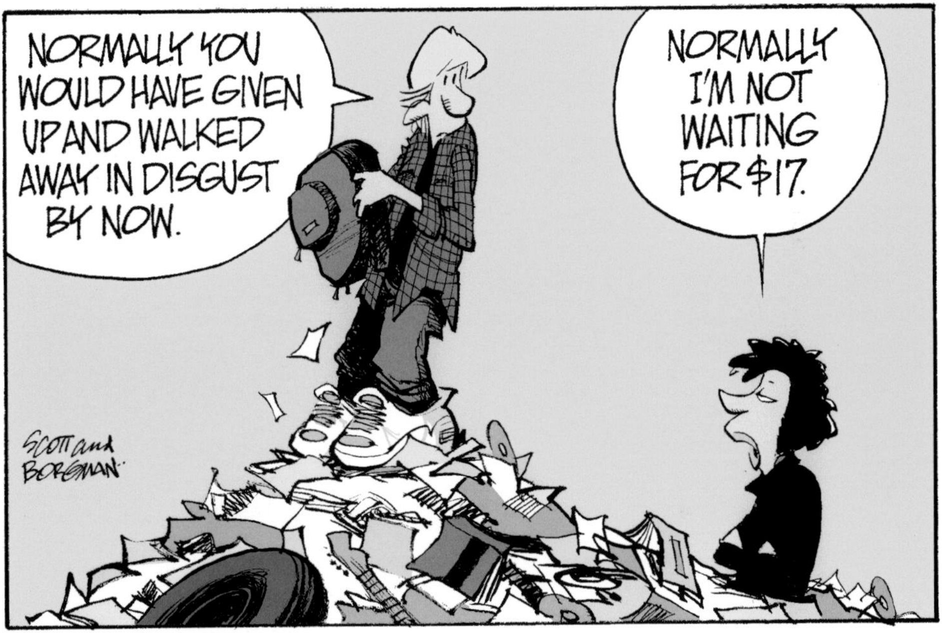
NORMALLY YOU WOULD HAVE GIVEN UP AND WALKED AWAY IN DISGUST BY NOW.
NORMALLY I'M NOT WAITING FOR $17.
SCOTT and BORGMAN

Stay sharp. They're counting on your failing memory.

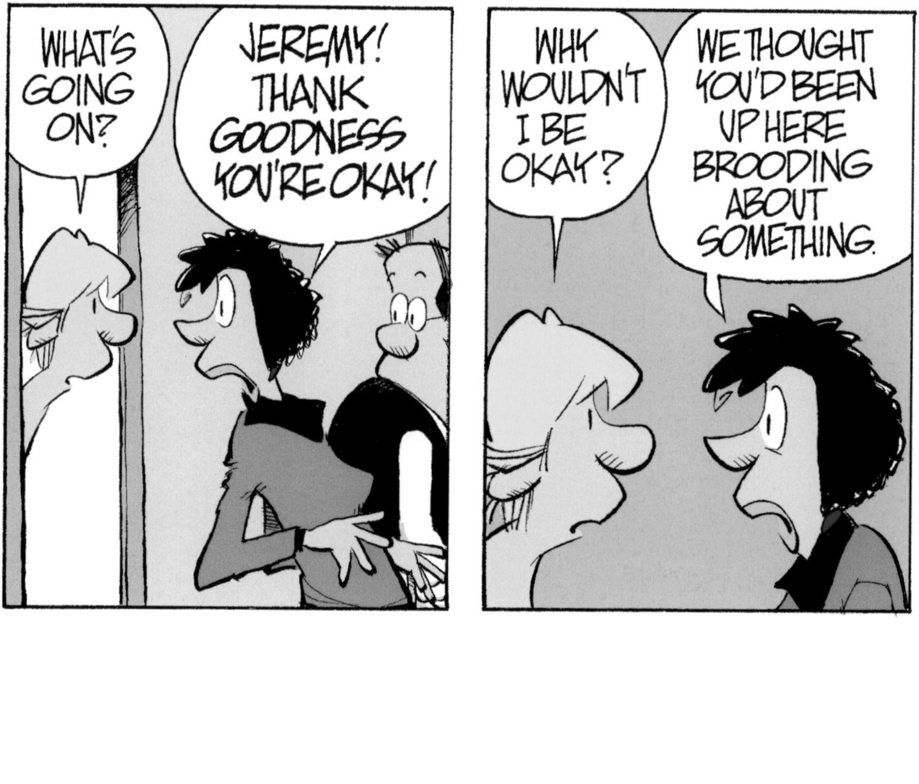
WHAT'S GOING ON?
JEREMY! THANK GOODNESS YOU'RE OKAY!
WHY WOULDN'T I BE OKAY?
WE THOUGHT YOU'D BEEN UP HERE BROODING ABOUT SOMETHING.

WHAT? THAT'S CRAZY!
WELL, WHERE HAVE YOU BEEN FOR THE LAST FIVE HOURS?
IN THE SHOWER.
SCOTT and BORGMAN

You may well have taken your last warm shower.

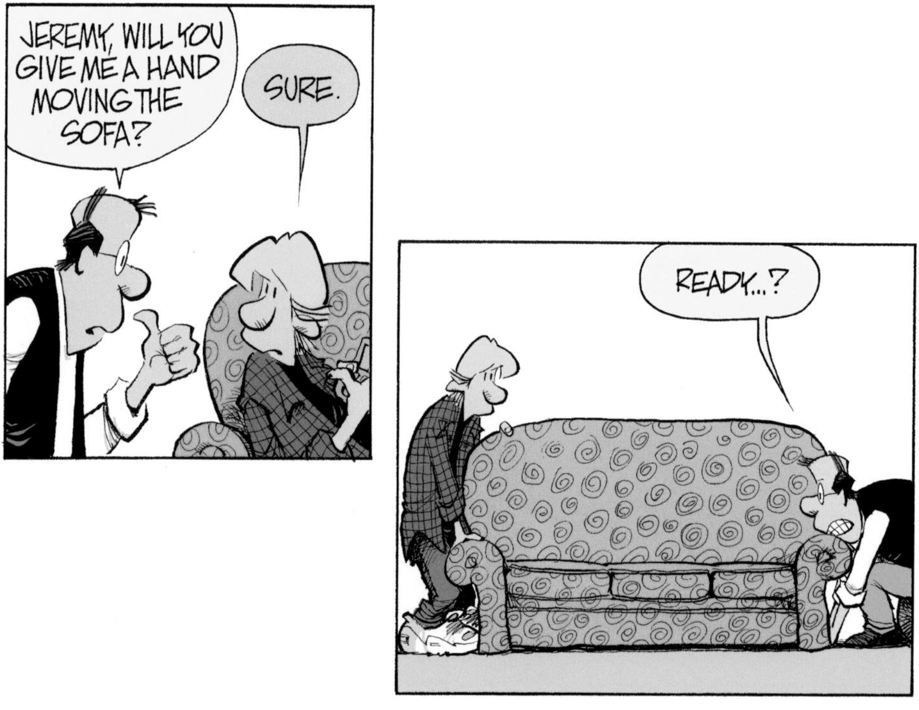
JEREMY, WILL YOU GIVE ME A HAND MOVING THE SOFA?
SURE.
READY...?

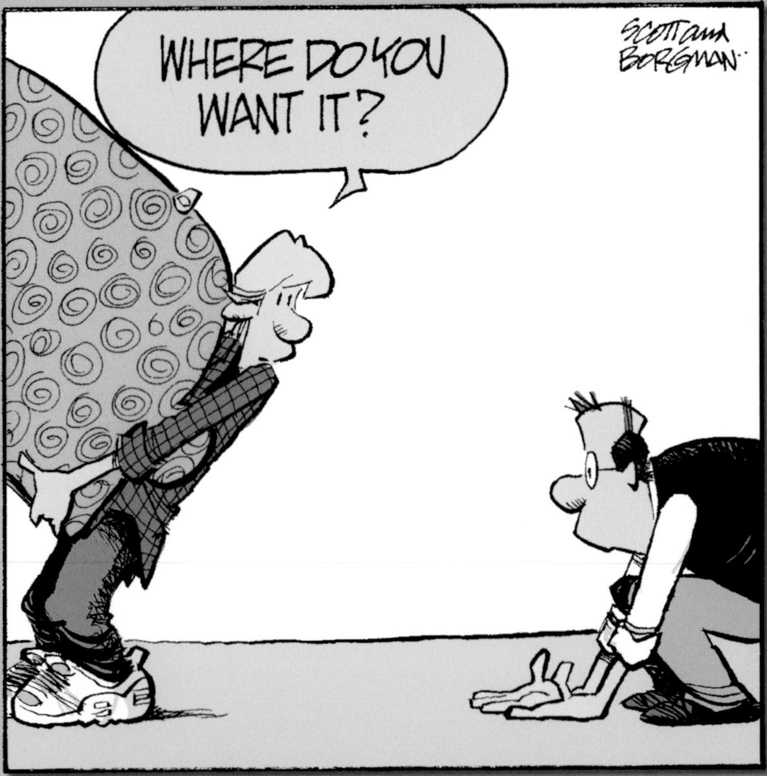
WHERE DO YOU WANT IT?
SCOTT and BORGMAN

One day you're carrying them over your shoulder, the next day they're mocking the way your knees crack when you walk across the room.

MAYBE IT'S NOT THAT BAD...
YOU LIKE THIS COLOR??
IT'S A LITTLE ANNOYING BUT I CAN LIVE WITH IT.
HOW CAN YOU LIVE WITH SOMETHING THAT CONSTANTLY ANNOYS YOU?

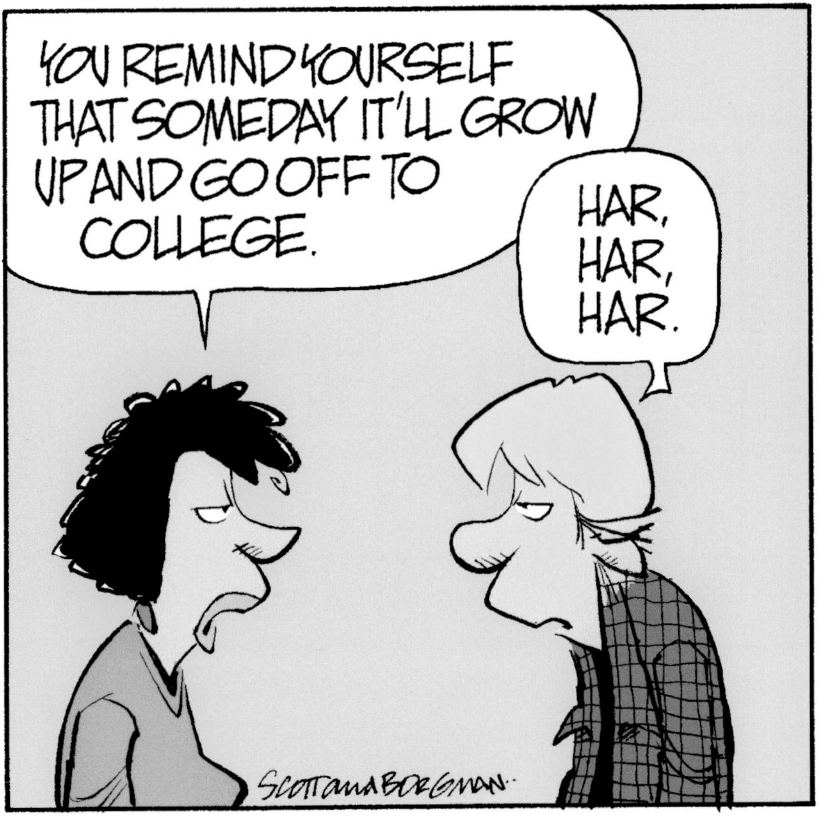
YOU REMIND YOURSELF THAT SOMEDAY IT'LL GROW UP AND GO OFF TO COLLEGE.
HAR, HAR, HAR.
SCOTT and BORGMAN

Your new goal is to live long enough for them to grow up and come back to apologize to you.

WHAT WERE YOU DOING IN THE BASEMENT, JEREMY?
IT'S LAUNDRY DAY.
GREAT! HOW MANY LOADS ARE YOU DOING?
ONE.

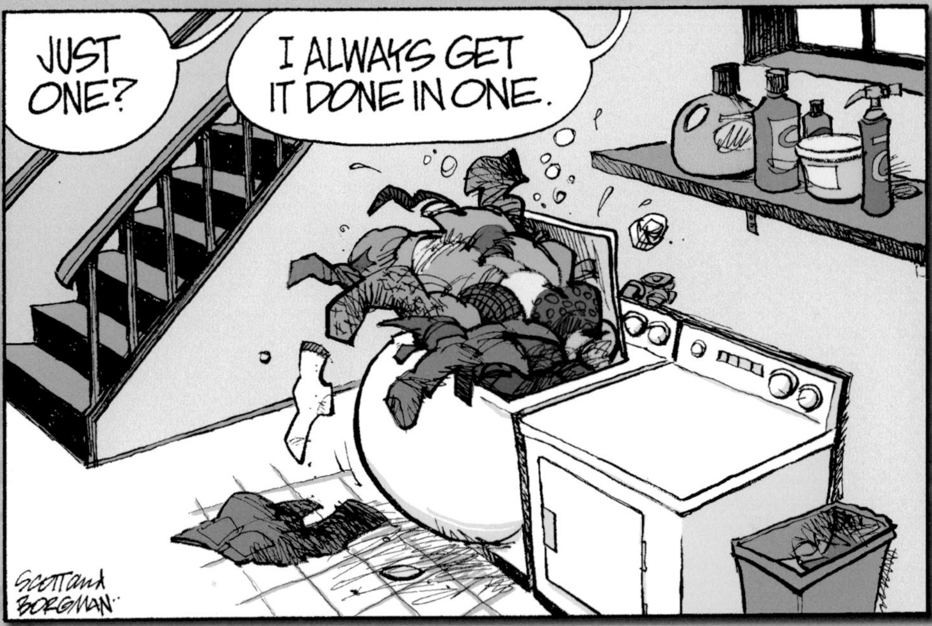
JUST ONE?
I ALWAYS GET IT DONE IN ONE.
SCOTT and BORGMAN

Encourage independence. And always buy the extended warranty.

MIND IF I JOIN YOU GUYS?
NOT AT ALL!
GREAT...

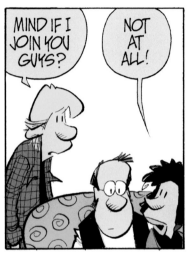

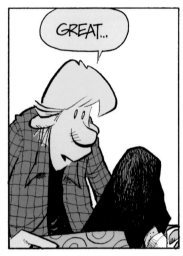

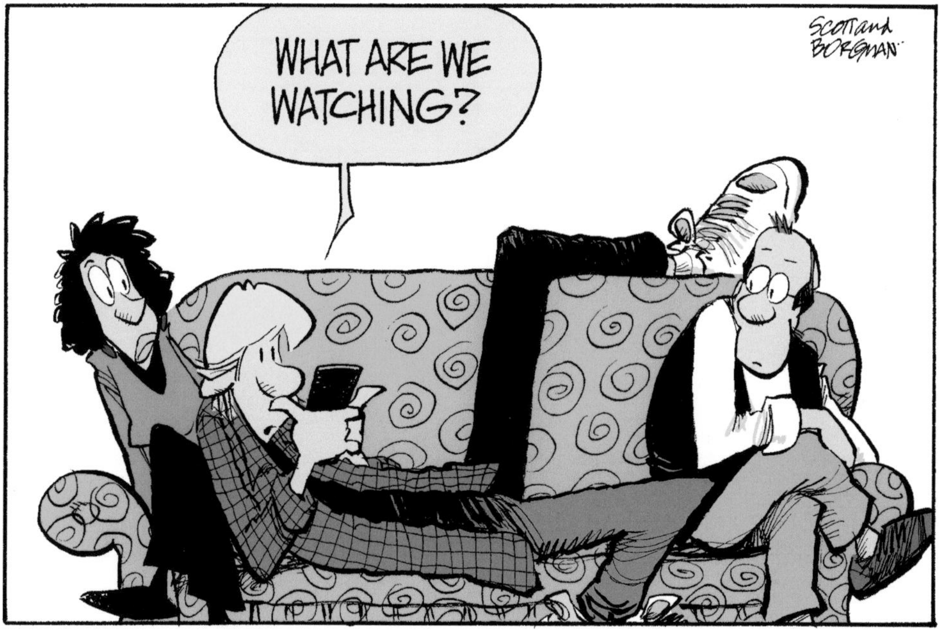
WHAT ARE WE WATCHING?
SCOTT and BORGMAN

Your teenager will occupy a lot of your time and most of your couch.

YAWN!
BRUSH! BRUSH! BRUSH!

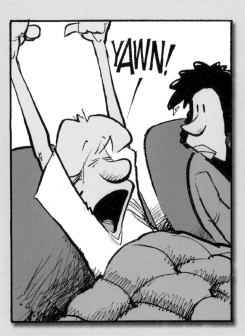

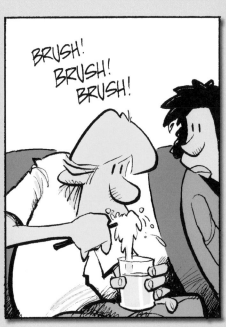

SCOTT and BORGMAN
ROLL! ROLL! ROLL!
MAYBE IF YOU WENT TO BED EARLIER, YOU WOULDN'T NEED TO SLEEP SO LATE!
SWISH! SWISH! SWISH!

Don't think of it as your car. Think of it as a pre–dorm room.

HOW DO YOU ALWAYS KNOW WHERE I AM??
I CALL IT DEBRIS-BASED INTUITION.

Use all of the tools at your disposal.

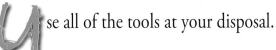

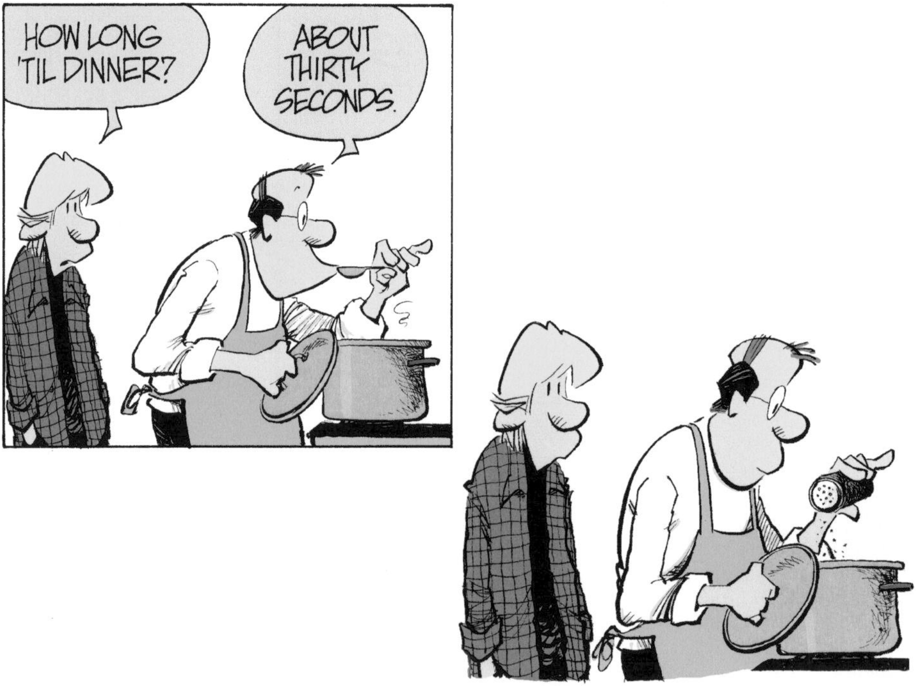
HOW LONG 'TIL DINNER?
ABOUT THIRTY SECONDS.

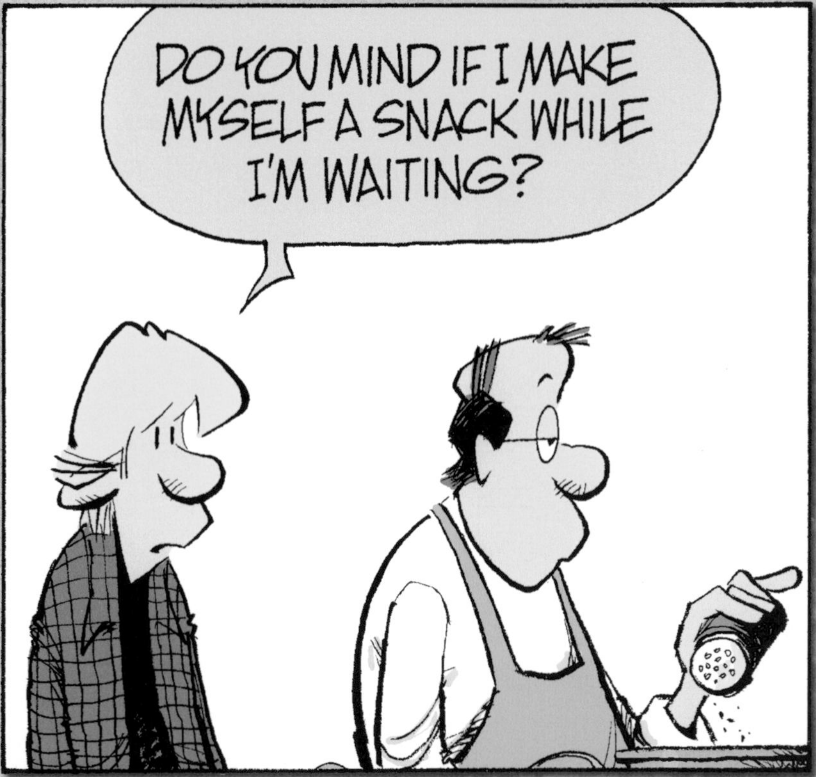
DO YOU MIND IF I MAKE MYSELF A SNACK WHILE I'M WAITING?

When they say, "I'm hungry," stand back.

MOM, CAN I HAVE SOME LUNCH MONEY?
JEREMY, YOU HAD LUNCH FIFTEEN MINUTES AGO!
OH, YEAH.

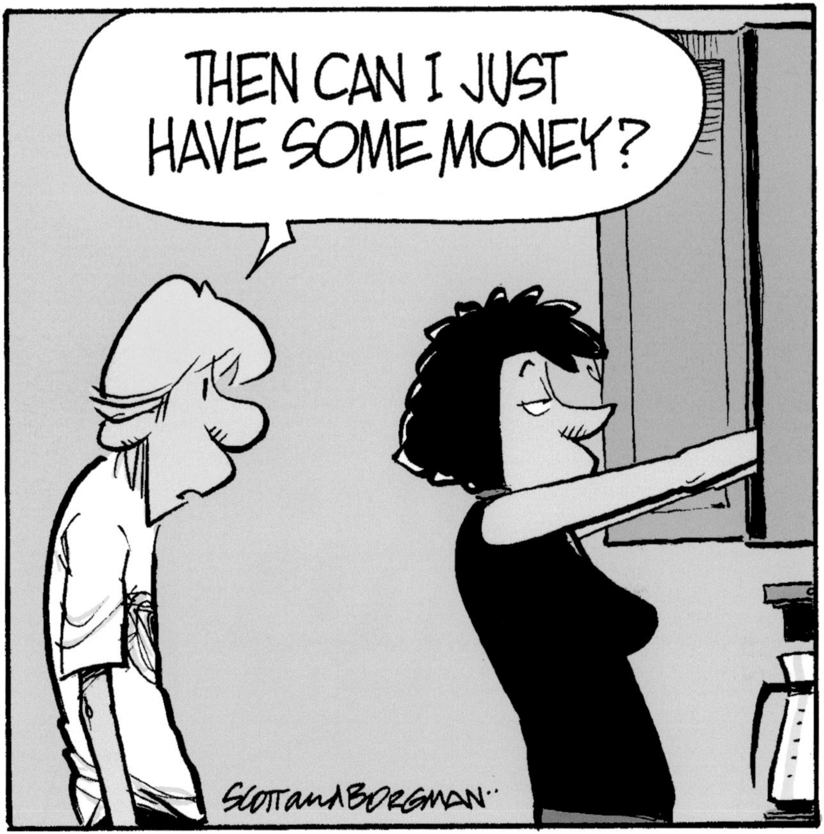
THEN CAN I JUST HAVE SOME MONEY?
SCOTT and BORGMAN

Learn to love the sheer chutzpah.

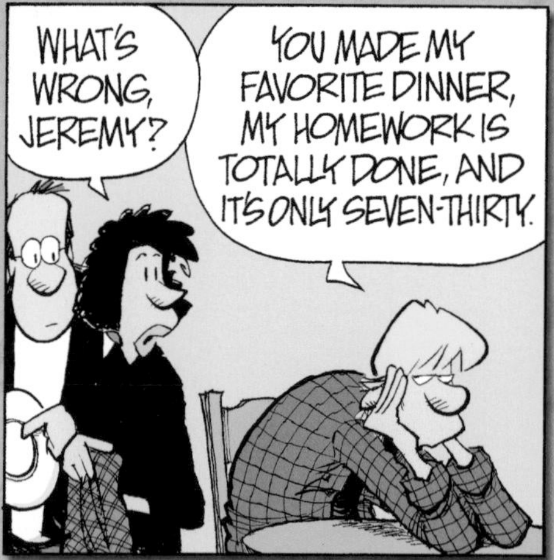
WHAT'S WRONG, JEREMY?
YOU MADE MY FAVORITE DINNER, MY HOMEWORK IS TOTALLY DONE, AND IT'S ONLY SEVEN-THIRTY.

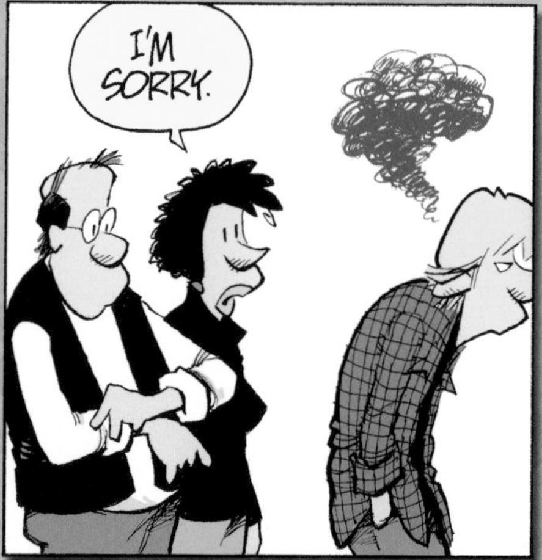
I'M SORRY.

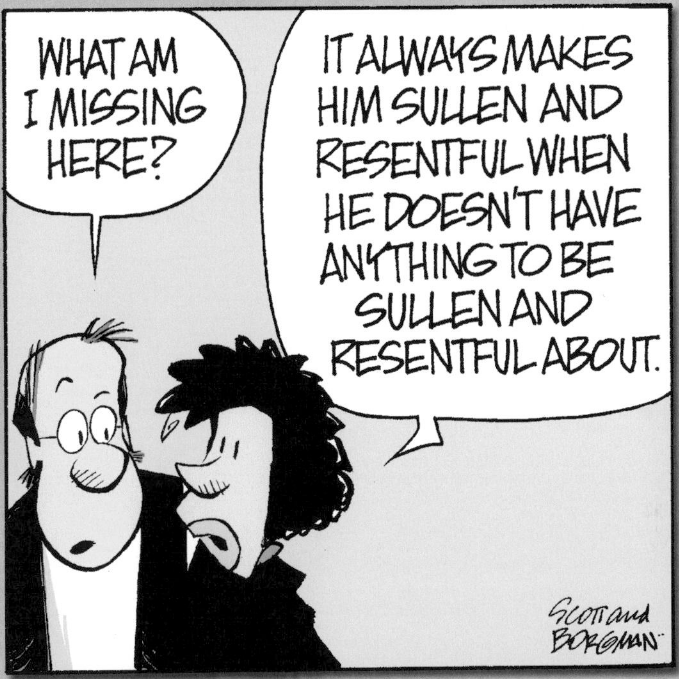
WHAT AM I MISSING HERE?
IT ALWAYS MAKES HIM SULLEN AND RESENTFUL WHEN HE DOESN'T HAVE ANYTHING TO BE SULLEN AND RESENTFUL ABOUT.
SCOTT and BORGMAN

"Sullen" and "resentful" will be your teenager's new baseline moods.

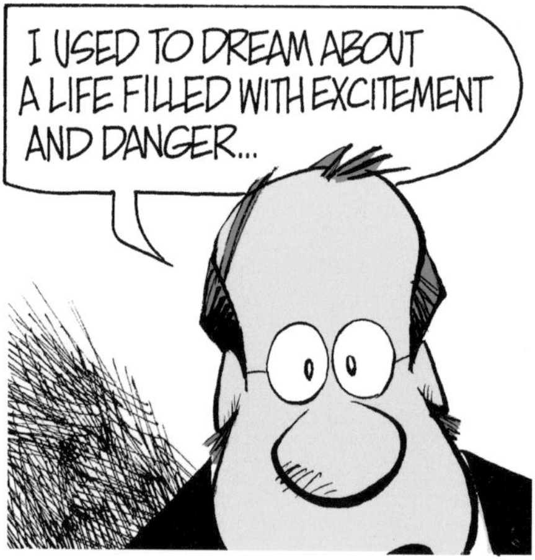
I USED TO DREAM ABOUT A LIFE FILLED WITH EXCITEMENT AND DANGER...

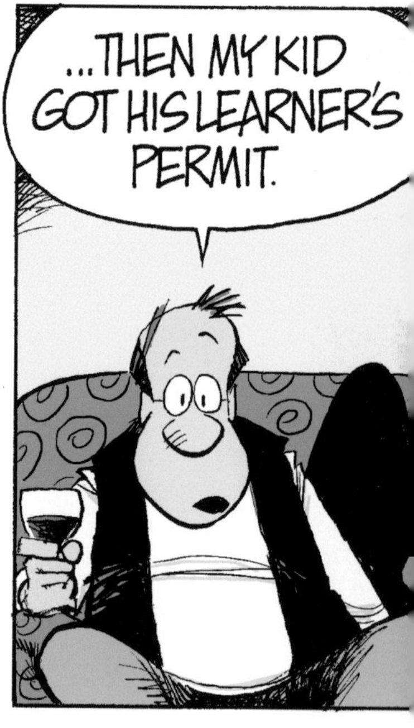
...THEN MY KID GOT HIS LEARNER'S PERMIT.

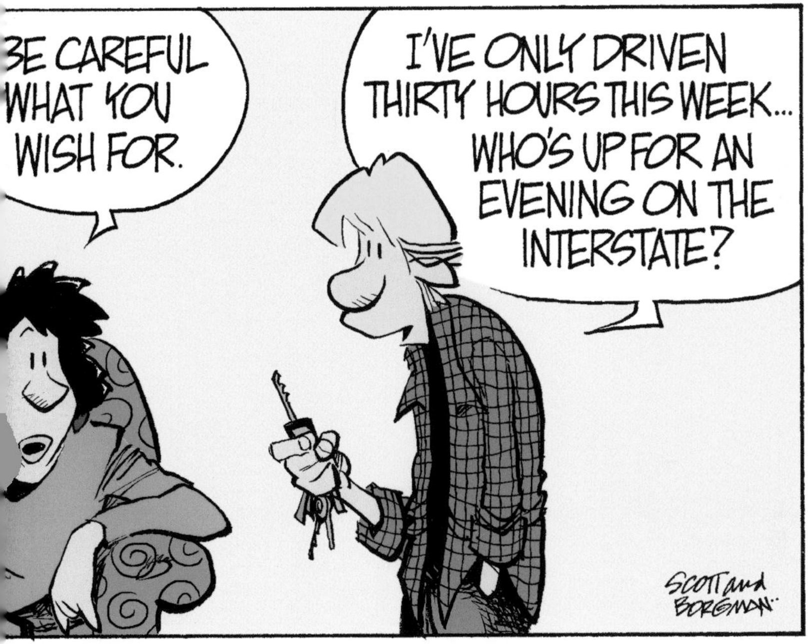
BE CAREFUL WHAT YOU WISH FOR.
I'VE ONLY DRIVEN THIRTY HOURS THIS WEEK... WHO'S UP FOR AN EVENING ON THE INTERSTATE?
SCOTT and BORGMAN

James Bond never had to brave life from the passenger's seat.

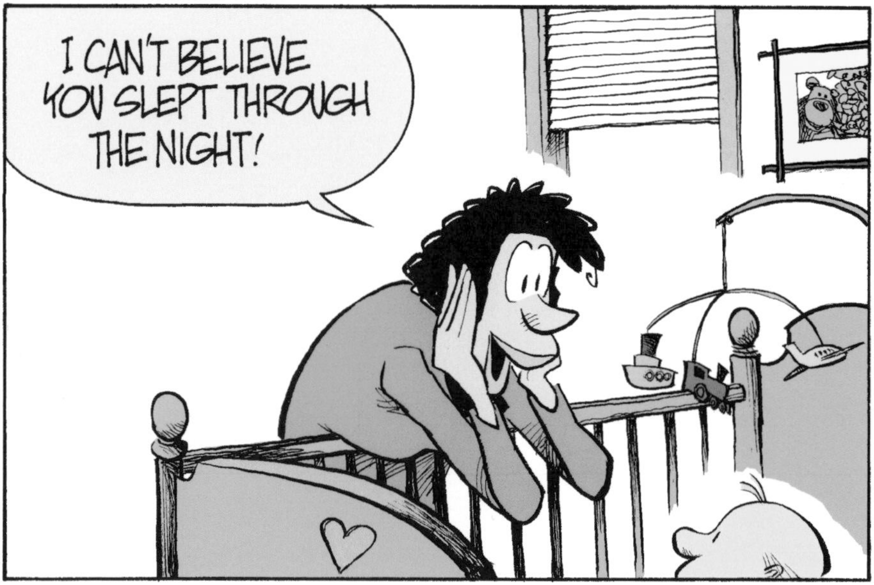
I CAN'T BELIEVE YOU SLEPT THROUGH THE NIGHT!

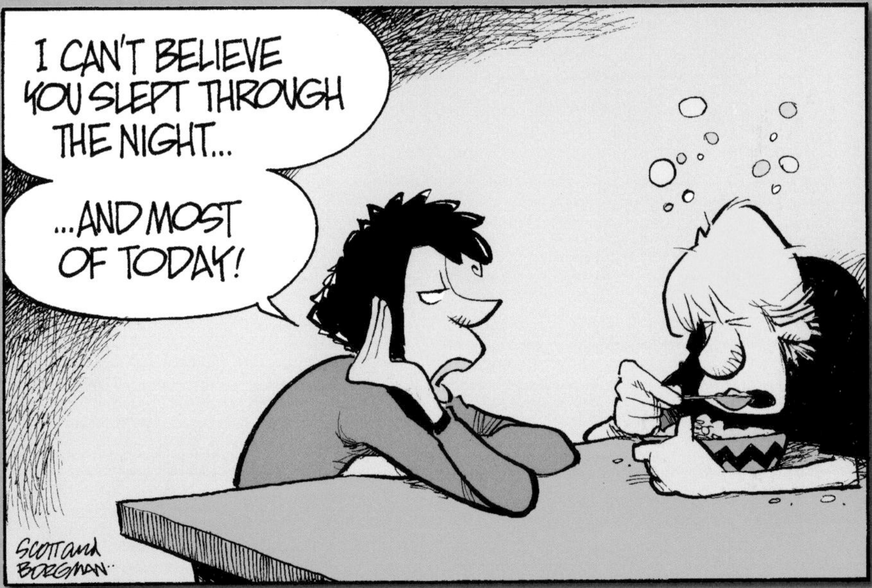
I CAN'T BELIEVE YOU SLEPT THROUGH THE NIGHT...
...AND MOST OF TODAY!
SCOTT and BORGMAN

The goalposts have moved.

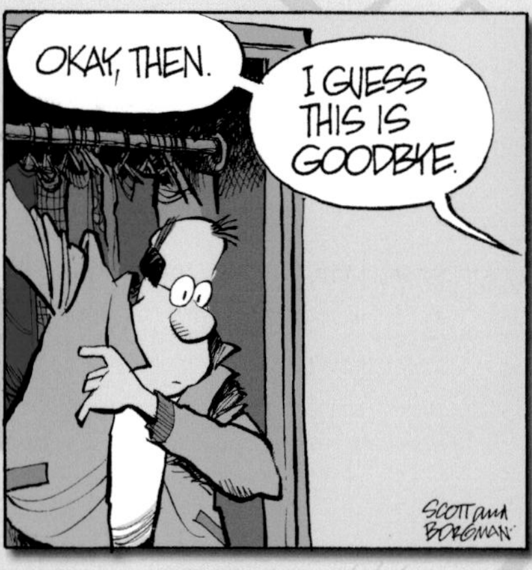
OKAY, THEN.
I GUESS THIS IS GOODBYE.
SCOTT and BORGMAN

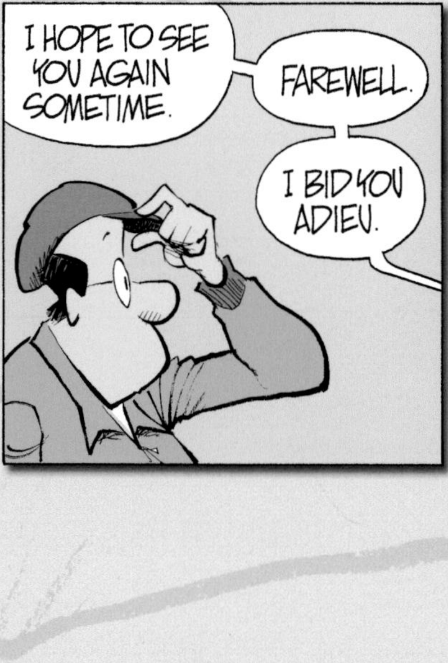
I HOPE TO SEE YOU AGAIN SOMETIME.
FAREWELL.
I BID YOU ADIEU.

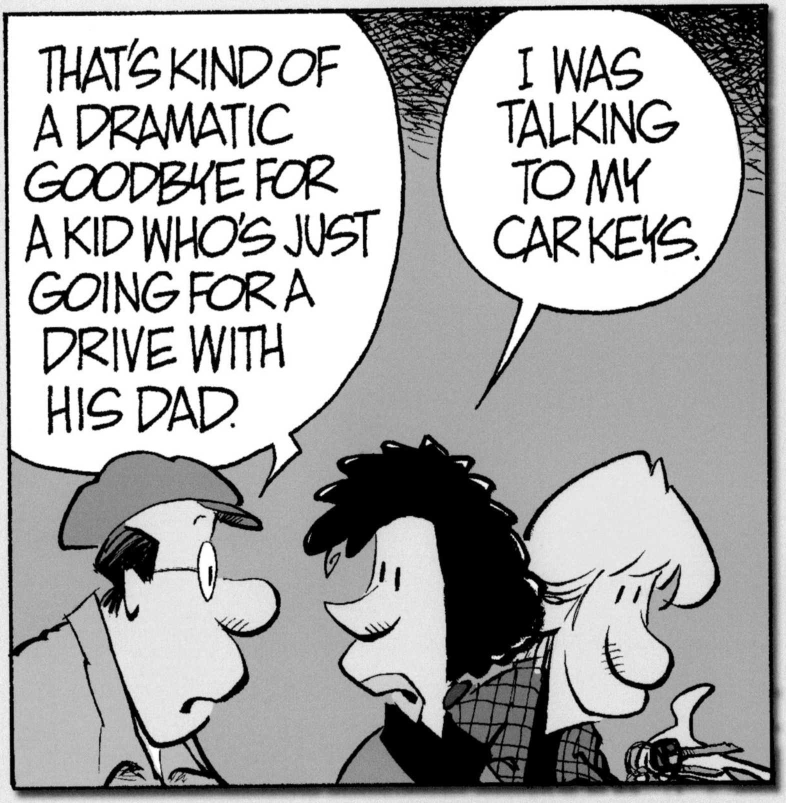
THAT'S KIND OF A DRAMATIC GOODBYE FOR A KID WHO'S JUST GOING FOR A DRIVE WITH HIS DAD.
I WAS TALKING TO MY CAR KEYS.

Free yourself from all earthly possessions . . . especially cups, dishes, telephone handsets, and anything clearly labeled "Do Not Touch."

I DON'T KNOW WHAT HAPPENED!
IT'S LIKE I WAS IN SOMEONE ELSE'S BODY.
ONE MINUTE I'M LYING IN BED, AND THE NEXT MINUTE I'M DRIVING YOUR CAR AROUND IN THE MIDDLE OF THE NIGHT TRYING TO IMPRESS A GIRL!
SCOTT and BORGMAN

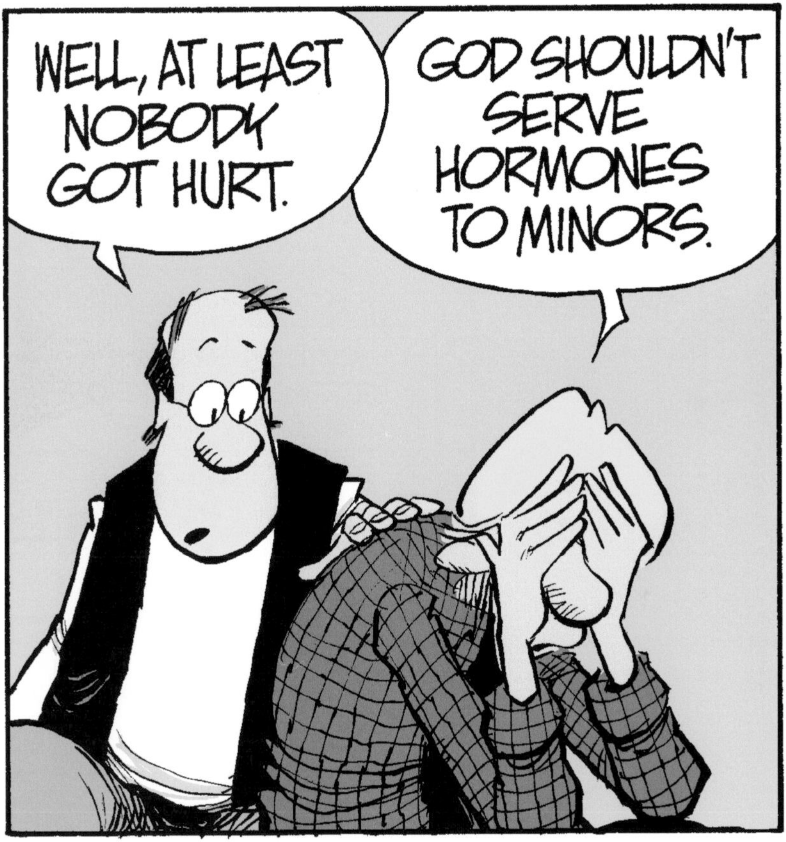
WELL, AT LEAST NOBODY GOT HURT.
GOD SHOULDN'T SERVE HORMONES TO MINORS.

Remember that the only one more confused by these years than you is your teenager.

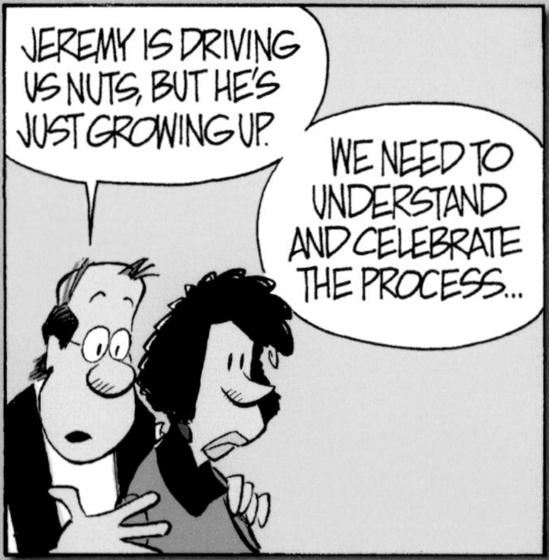
JEREMY IS DRIVING US NUTS, BUT HE'S JUST GROWING UP.
WE NEED TO UNDERSTAND AND CELEBRATE THE PROCESS...

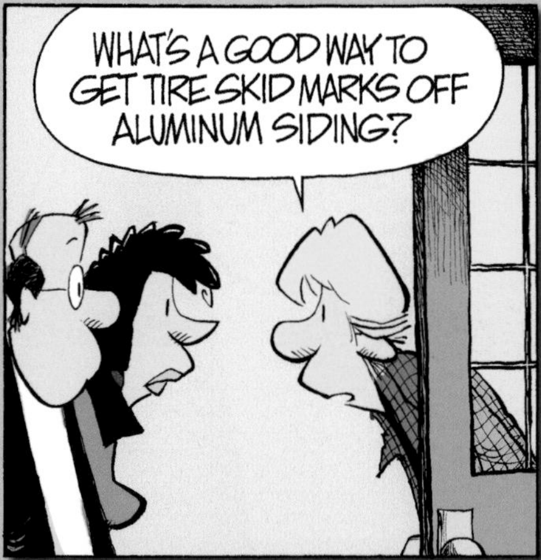
WHAT'S A GOOD WAY TO GET TIRE SKID MARKS OFF ALUMINUM SIDING?

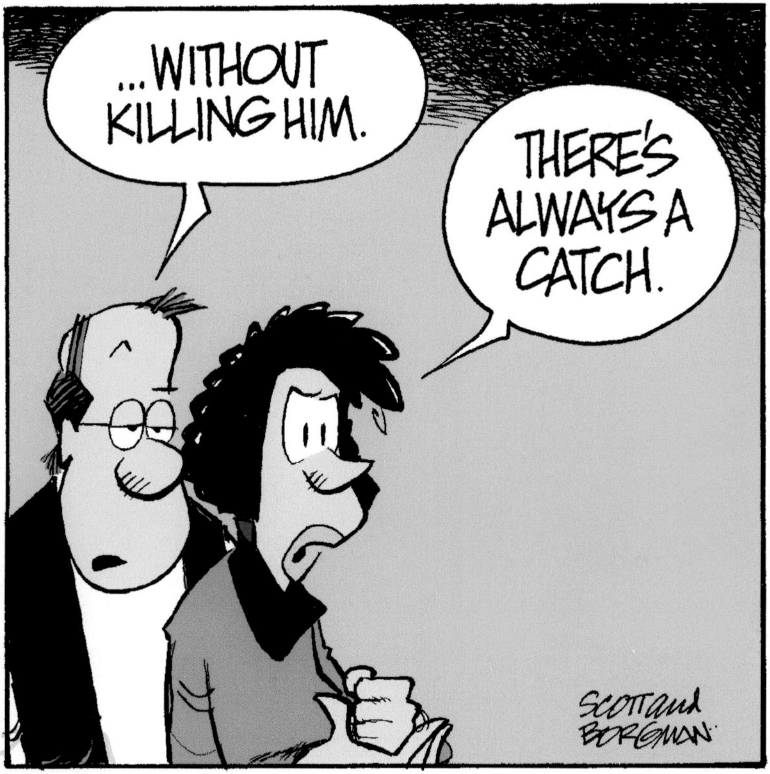
...WITHOUT KILLING HIM.
THERE'S ALWAYS A CATCH.
SCOTT and BORGMAN

Teenagers launch themselves by planting their feet firmly on your chest and pushing off.

MOM! THERE AREN'T ANY CLEAN TOWELS IN MY ROOM!
I JUST HAD TO DRY OFF WITH A BAG OF COTTON BALLS AND SOME POCKET LINT!
I HANDED YOU A STACK OF CLEAN TOWELS TWO DAYS AGO, AND THEY'RE STILL SITTING THERE ON THE STAIRS WHERE YOU LEFT THEM!

OH SURE, EVERYTHING'S MY FAULT.
SCOTT and BORGMAN

But rest assured, no matter how much chaos your teenager causes, somehow it will always be your fault.

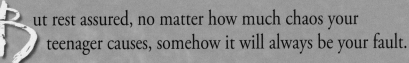

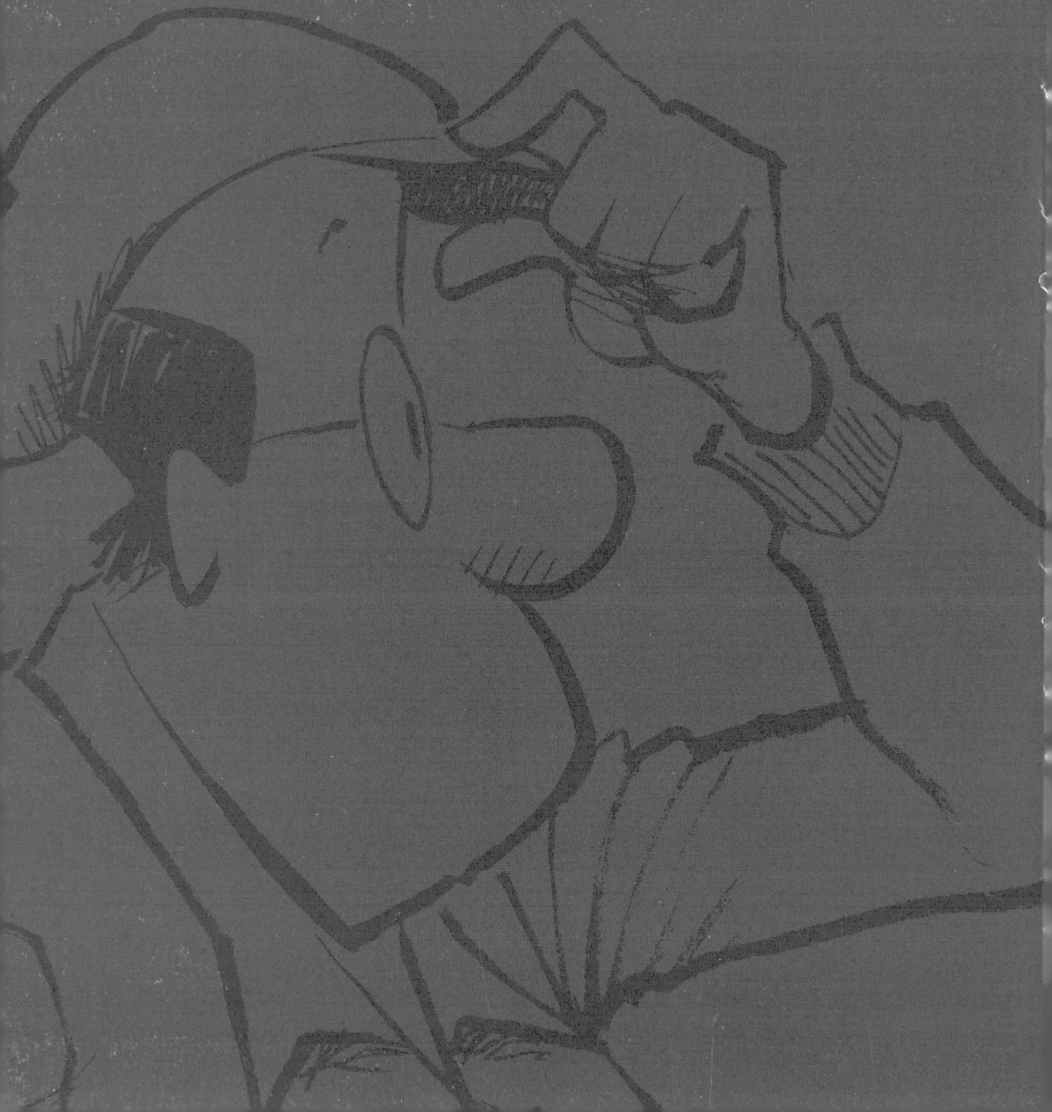